LEARN TO SPEAK PORTUGUESE
(WITHOUT EVEN TRYING)

Stephen Hernandez

Copyright © 2020 by Stephen Hernandez

All rights reserved. No part of this publication may be reproduced, distributed or transmitted in any form or by any means, without prior written permission.

www.stephenhernandez.co.uk

Publisher's Note: This is a work of non-fiction. Locales and public names are sometimes used for atmospheric purposes. Businesses, companies, events, institutions, and locales that are mentioned are duly referenced and used in context only.

Book Layout © 2017 BookDesignTemplates.com

ISBN: 978-1-9161126-6-7

Learn to Speak Portuguese / Stephen Hernandez. -- 1st ed.

To all my subscribers at:

https://stephenhernandez.co.uk/

A new language is a new life.

—PERSIAN PROVERB

CONTENTS

Introduction to learning Portuguese	P.7
1. Learning at home	P16
2. Learning Portuguese on your own	P36
3. Practicing Portuguese on your own	P40
4. A guide for the complete beginner	P54
5. Fluency	P64
6. Forgetting	P66
7. Portuguese grammar	P94
8. Motivation	P100
9. Best Portuguese TV shows	P108
10. Navigating the restaurant	P127
11. Partying	P134
12. Travel	P140
13. Learning like a child	P148
14. Speaking Portuguese	P153
15. Learning without trying	P196
Conclusion	P207
Bibliography & online resources	P208

INTRODUCTION

LEARNING PORTUGUESE

The purpose of this book is to teach you *how* to learn, rather than what to learn. It would be impossible to discuss the Portuguese language's complete grammatical structure and, every Portuguese word and its correct pronunciation in one book and if ever such a book were written it would be incredibly tedious. The aim of this book is to get you speaking Portuguese to the extent you can hold a reasonable conversation with a native speaker and you can read and understand a newspaper and magazine article written in Portuguese, be it Portugal Portuguese or Brazilian Portuguese. Once you have progressed that far you will not need the help of any book, course, or teacher—you will just need to practice.

Make no mistake—learning a language when you are not living in a country where it is spoken is very difficult. Not only do you not have situations where you can practice your new found learning but you are constantly bombarded by your native language as soon as you leave the classroom or your chosen place of learning. In many ways it becomes a case of perseverance. I liken it to the starting of a new exercise regime. You enroll in a local gym (giving you the added incentive that you are actually paying to get fitter). At first you are full of enthusiasm and energy so you set yourself unrealistic goals. Instead of starting off walking and progressing to running, you start off at a mad sprint and quickly tire. The novelty soon wears off and going to the gym becomes an irksome duty. Then excuses for not going begin to kick in, and before you know it you have given up altogether.

- Absolutely anyone can learn Portuguese.
- I'm completely serious.

It doesn't matter what your excuse is. Maybe you think you stink at languages. Maybe you think you're too lazy. Maybe you flunked out of high school Portuguese or maybe you just can't pronounce the word *obrigado* (thank you) no matter how hard you try.

If you really want to learn Portuguese, **you can do it.** Best of all you can do it without even trying. The only effort you have to make is to read this book (and even then you can skip the bits you don't like), make a concrete plan to study (one you can stick to), keep it fun (extremely important), and stay motivated over the long haul (self-explanatory).

- Decide on a simple, attainable goal to start with so that you don't feel overwhelmed.
- Make learning Portuguese a lifestyle change.

- Invite Portuguese into your daily life. That way, your brain will consider it something useful and worth caring about.
- Let technology help you out. The internet is absolutely great for learning Portuguese—use it.
- Think about learning Portuguese as a gateway to new experiences. Think of the fun things you want to do and turn them into language-learning opportunities.
- Make new friends. Interacting in Portuguese is key—it will teach you to intuitively express your thoughts, instead of mentally translating each sentence before you say it. If you are a bit shy about getting the ball rolling with native speakers nearby, you can do this online (there is a whole chapter on this).
- Most of all do not worry about making mistakes. One of the most common barriers to conversing in a new language is the fear of making mistakes. But native speakers are like doting parents: any attempt from you to communicate in their language is objective proof that you are some sort of gifted genius. They'll appreciate your effort and even help you. The more you speak, the closer you'll get to the elusive ideal of "native fluency."

To start off with don't set yourself unrealistic goals or a grandiose study plan. Keep it simple. Set aside a small amount of time that you can reasonably spare even if it just means getting up 15 minutes earlier in the morning. If you set that time aside and avoid distractions that 15 minutes will be invaluable. Above all make it as fun as possible. No one said learning a new language was easy but neither should it be irksome.

You can use this book in tandem with any other learning resource you may be using at the moment if that resource is working for you. At some point, though, you will find you have your own particular way of learning, and discovering that is very important. Once you find what works, you will have achieved an important milestone, and your learning will accelerate accordingly. I hope that with this book you will find your "way" sooner rather than later. That is what I designed it to do.

This book has no strict order (you can jump to and from chapters if you want), no particular rules to follow, and I definitely do not take anything for granted except the fact that you want to learn to speak Portuguese and most probably want the experience to be as painless as possible.

I should make one thing clear from the beginning this book is not designed to "teach" you Portuguese. It is designed to help you learn how to teach yourself to "speak" Portuguese with the least effort possible. It gives you a process and pointers on how to learn to speak Portuguese effectively. Consider it an autodidactic guide.

It is also a guide to learning subconsciously. By subconsciously, I do not mean that you go to sleep listening to tapes in Portuguese or practice some kind of self-hypnosis. What we are aiming at is picking up Portuguese without forcing the issue. The greatest aim in learning any language is being able to think in that language and not be aware that you are doing it. Stick with me and you will obtain that goal.

Sound impossible? It won't be by the time you have finished this book.

A journey of a thousand miles begins with a single step.

Yeah, we've all heard that one from a thousand language teachers.

As far as advice goes, that saying is about as useful as an ashtray on a motorbike.

Think about it. If you're stranded in a foreign wilderness with no idea about *how* to get where you want to go, you'll have an extraordinarily difficult time getting there no matter how many footsteps you take. In fact, you'll probably end up going around in circles.

But if you've got a map and compass, as well as some decent navigating skills, you're likely to be on your way a lot faster.

In the same way, when you're starting to learn a new language, it helps to have a road map to both guide you along and guarantee that you're still headed in the right direction when you get stuck or feel lost.

Just like physical maps, a map for language learning should be based on what other people have seen. There are a number of polyglots and dedicated language learners out there who have become cartographers of the linguistic frontier. We will be drawing on their collective experience.

We will take this collective language learning experience, along with some scientific and technical know-how, and set out on the path to learning a new language in double time.

Here are some basic strategies to get you started:

- Become your own coach—develop goals and strategies. If you have heard of bullet journals, now is a good time to put one into practice. If this fails to ring the smallest of bells in the lockers of your memory, Google it and decide if you like the idea—it comes in very handy when learning a new language.
- A lot of the time, when we start something new, we make vague statements like, "I want to be able to speak well as quickly as possible," or, "I'm going to study Portuguese as much as I possibly can." This can be a problem because, when we create such vague goals, it can be very difficult to achieve any sort of meaningful result. That's why orienting your Portuguese learning odyssey should start with the use of two techniques: **SMART goals** and **metacognitive strategies**.
- **SMART,** in this case, is an acronym that means **S**pecific, **M**easurable, **A**chievable, **R**esults, **T**ime-bound. The synopsis of this is that you need to make really, really concrete goals that can be

achieved (even if you're incredibly lazy—see next chapter). Setting realistic goals like this is an essential skill for anyone studying by themselves, as well as anyone who wishes to maximize their study time.
- **Metacognitive strategies** involves three steps. First, you plan. Ask yourself what your specific goals are and what strategies you're going to use to achieve them. Second, start learning and keep track of how well you do every day. Are you having problems that need new solutions? Write that down. Are you consistently succeeding or failing in a certain area? Keep track of that, too. And the third and final step, after a few weeks to a month, it is time to **evaluate yourself**. Were you able to achieve your goals? If not, why? What strategies did and didn't work? Then the whole process repeats again.

These two techniques naturally fit together quite well, and they're both indispensable for making sure you're cooking with gas every time you sit or lie down to study.

Total immersion (i.e., living in a Portuguese speaking country) and speaking, seeing, hearing, reading and writing it all the time is, of course, the ultimate way to learn and is certainly the ultimate goal to strive for. Most of us aren't free to move from country to country as we please and must make decisions about when the best time would be for us to go to that oh-so-wonderful country we've been daydreaming about for countless hours. So, this book is aimed mainly at people who are studying from home in their native country.

Enjoy yourself.
Languages can be difficult to master. Even the easiest of languages for English speakers can take six hundred hours to conquer, according to the Foreign Service Institute, and perhaps much more than that if you want to do something with it professionally. This is not something you can do day in, day out without getting some pleasure out of the whole *ordeal*.

Thankfully, language is as human an obstacle as it gets and is naturally tied to amazing and fulfilling rewards. Think about how wonderful it is or could be to read your favorite Portuguese or Brazilian author in the original, or understand a Portuguese or Brazilian film without having to look at the sub-titles, or most amazing of all, hold a conversation with someone in their native language! Language is the thing that connects us to other people and the social benefits are extremely powerful.

Just think about how often you check Facebook. Why are social networking sites so popular? Because any information connected to other people is inherently seductive. So, from the get-go, make sure that you use your language skills for what they were made for—socializing.

Sometimes, when your schedule is crazy, you'll be tempted to jettison the "fun" things that made you attracted to learning Portuguese in the first place to get some regular practice in. Maybe you'll skip your favorite Portuguese TV show or Brazilian soap because you can't understand it without subtitles yet (more on this later), or you'll forget to keep up with the latest news on your favorite Brazilian samba band.

Make time for the things that got you started. They're what motivate you and push you through when language learning seems like a brutal punishment.

Really, it's all about balance. The steps are all here, laid out for you.

Only by starting out on the journey will you gain intuitive control, the sense of masterful dexterity like that of a professional athlete or a samurai warrior.

You have your map.

Now you just need to take those first steps ...

CHAPTER ONE

LEARNING AT HOME
(even if you're really lazy)

Do you have hopes and dreams of speaking a language fluently, but you're too lazy to study?

So do many people, but they give up before they've even started because it just seems like so much effort towards an intangible goal. And seriously—who *wants* to study?

But what if I told you that your laziness, far from being a limitation, could actually make you great at learning Portuguese?

Read on (if you can be bothered) to find out why the lazy way is often the best way and learn ways you can leverage your laziness to learn a language effectively at home.

Lazy people find better ways to do things

If you were a builder at the end of the 19th century, life was hard. Long hours. Bad pay. Little regard for health and safety. If you were really unlucky, it could even cost you your life: five men died during the construction of the Empire State

Building, and 27 died working on the Brooklyn Bridge. Mortality rates amongst builders in Victorian Britain were even more horrendous. In short, being a builder was a dangerous job.

What qualities did builders need in such a demanding and dangerous job?

Tenacity? Diligence? Stamina?

No. Not at all.

In 1868, a young construction worker named Frank Gilbreth, while observing colleagues to understand why some bricklayers were more effective than others, made a startling discovery.

The best builders weren't those who tried the hardest. The men Gilbreth learned the most from were the laziest ones.

Laying bricks requires repeating the same skilled movements over and over again: the fewer motions, the better. In an attempt to conserve energy, the "lazy" builders had found ways to lay bricks with a minimum number of motions. In short, they'd found more effective ways to get the job done.

But what do lazy bricklayers have to do with learning Portuguese, apart from the fact that I worked as one for a while? (I wasn't very good at laying bricks, but I was excellent at being lazy!)

Well, inspired by his lazy colleagues, Gilbreth went on to pioneer "time and motion study," a technique that streamlines work systems and is still used today in many fields to increase productivity. You know that person in the operating room who passes scalpels to the surgeon and wipes their brow? Gilbreth came up with that idea.

Hiring someone to pass you things from 20 centimeters away and wipe the sweat off your own forehead? It doesn't get much lazier than that. Yet it helps surgeons work more efficiently and probably saves lives in the process.

The bottom line? The lazy way is usually the smartest way.

Over the years, Gilbreth's ideas have been attributed to people like Bill Gates, who is (falsely) reported to have said: "I will always choose a lazy person to do a difficult job because he will find an easy way to do it." (This attribution, although factually incorrect, makes a nice motivational poster to hang in your office.)

The lazy way

One of the most embarrassing episodes in my life (and there are quite a few, believe me!) was when I unadvisedly went to a parents' evening at my young daughter's primary school. The teacher asked each child in turn what their fathers did for a living. My daughter's response: "He lies on the sofa with his hands down his trousers."

Actually, that is partly true, although you may be relieved to know that I don't spend *all* my time with my hands down my trousers. If there's one thing I love more than writing, listening to the radio, and browsing the web, it's sitting or lying on the sofa in my pants, reading or watching TV—a lot of the time in Portuguese. Fortunately, with regards to writing this book, these activities aren't mutually exclusive, so I'm always on the lookout for ways to combine my favorite pastimes.

I've scoured the web to find the best resources to learn Portuguese, and this book contains my findings. Hopefully, the information contained herein will save you a lot of time and money spent on useless systems and pointless exercises and will repay your faith in me. When you speak Portuguese (which you will), please remember to recommend it to your friends. Even if you don't use a computer, there is enough basic information here to get you started on your path to learning Portuguese. But I would strongly advise getting on the internet if you intend to learn from home with some degree of success.

If your school was anything like mine, you may have some experience learning languages with the "try harder" approach: page after page of grammar exercises, long vocabulary lists, listening exercises about stationary or some other excruciatingly boring topic. And if you still can't speak the language after all that effort? Well, you should try harder.

But what if there's a better way to learn a language? A lazier way, that you can use to learn a language at home and, with less effort?

A way to learn by doing things you actually enjoy? A way to learn by having a laugh with native speakers? A way to learn without taking your pajamas off?

There is.

Don't get me wrong. Languages take time and effort; there's no getting around that. This isn't about being idle.

It's about finding effective ways to learn (remember: SMART and metacognitive strategies?) so you can stop wasting time and energy on stuff that doesn't work. With that in mind, I've put together a collection of lazy (but highly effective) ways to learn a language at home or away.

They'll help you:

- Speak a language better by studying less!
- Go against "traditional" language learning methods to get better results.
- Get fluent in a language while sitting around in your undies and drinking beer (this isn't compulsory).

Don't study (much).

A lot of people try to learn a language by "studying." They try really hard to memorize grammar rules and vocabulary in the hope that one day, all the pieces will come together and they'll magically start speaking the language.

Sorry, but languages don't work that way.

Trying to speak a language by doing grammar exercises is like trying to make bread by reading cookbooks. Sure, you'll pick up some tips, but you'll never learn how to bake unless you're willing to get your hands dirty.

Languages are a learn-by-doing kind of a deal. The best way to learn to speak, understand, read, and write a language is by practicing speaking, listening, reading, and writing. That doesn't mean you should never study grammar or vocabulary. It helps to get an idea of how the language works. But if you dedicate a disproportionate amount of time to that stuff, it'll clutter your learning experience and hold you back from actually speaking Portuguese.

You'll learn much faster by *using the language.*

Now, if you're totally new to language learning, you may be wondering how you can start using a language you don't know yet. If you're learning completely from scratch, a good textbook can help you pick up the basics. But avoid ones that teach lots of grammar rules without showing you how to use them in real life. The best textbooks are the ones that give you lots of example conversations and introduce grammar in bite-size pieces.

As soon as you can, aim to get lots of exposure to the Portuguese language being used in a real way. If you're a lower-level learner, you can start by reading books that have been simplified for your level (called graded readers). Look for ones accompanied by audio so you can work on your listening at the same time.

If you can, keep a diary or journal of your experience with different methods of learning. Bullet journals are great for this. Never heard of them? They are basically a sort of a cross between a diary and a to-do list. Keeping one will help you see what works for you and what doesn't, and also to chart your progress. You can buy readymade ones to suit you or design your own. You can use it for motivation when you feel like you are getting nowhere, as you will see at a glance all the progress you have made. Believe me, you will be surprised at how far you have come and sometimes you just need a little reminder to give you that motivational push. You will also be able to see what areas you need to improve in and the types of things you are best at. When you are feeling low, go back to the stuff you are best at.

Consider how a child has learned to speak a language. Presumably, unless it was a precocious genius, it did not start off by reading a primer in grammar. Children start off by observing and identifying. Naming and pronunciation comes from hearing the description of the object from others, usually adults, or other kids fluent in the language.

This is something you can do right now, right this minute. Start off by naming in Portuguese the objects that surround you, write the Portuguese name for the object on a Post-it Note, and stick it on the object. You can find the Portuguese translation for any household object online or in a two-way dictionary. I would advise using an online dictionary if you can, as these usually include a guide to pronunciation that you can actually listen to without trying to do it phonetically.

Put the Post-it Note at eye level or some place you will encounter it immediately upon looking at the object. Begin by saying the objects name out loud—or, perhaps, if you have company, in your head. At this point, don't worry too much if your friends and family think you have gone a little crazy. You are learning a new language; they are not. Give yourself a pat on the back instead.

Below is a short list of some common things around the house to give you a start and the idea behind this method. Remember to write the name of the object in **Portuguese** only. Preferably, put your Post-it Note on an immovable object (your spouse or significant other might take exception to having a Post-it Note stuck on their forehead, and so might your dog or cat).

- Put the Post it Notes on everything in your house (use a two-way dictionary). It is a great way to learn nouns (the name of things). Portuguese nouns come in two types: masculine and feminine. Masculine nouns usually end in an -o, and feminine nouns usually end in an -a. The adjective's gender should match the gender of the noun. Soon you will begin to identify these objects in Portuguese without consciously thinking about it.

table	*tabela*
chair	*cadeira*
desk	*mesa*
window	*janela*
door	*porta*
wall	*parede*
bed	*cama*
blanket	*cobertor*
television	*televisão*
radio	*rádio*
stove	*fogão*
oven	*forno*
microwave	*microonda*
light	*luz*
garbage	*lixo*
carpet	*carpete*
cupboard	*armário de cozinha*
armchair	*poltrona*
refrigerator	*geladeria*
mirror	*espelho*

Examples:

- I put my book on the **table**.
- *Eu coloquei o meu livro sobre a* **mesa**.

- Mary turns on the **radio** to listen to music.
- *Maria liga o rádio para ouvir música.*

- You forgot to turn off the **television** yesterday.
- *Você se esqueceu de desligar a **televisão** ontem.*

- My uncle enjoys seeing the park by the **window**.
- *O meu tio gosta de ver o parque perto da **janela**.*

- Her little brother drew a tree on the **wall**.
- *Seu irmãozinho tirou uma árvore na **parede**.*

Why do you care whether a noun is masculine or feminine?

Good question! As you shall see later on, Portuguese places a great deal more emphasis on gender than does English.

Another great way to learn when you are feeling lazy is to listen to podcasts with transcripts and simplified, slowed speech. There is a whole chapter dedicated to this later on.

Sit around in your undies (just like The Naked Trader!)
Next, you'll need to practice speaking. Luckily, you can now do this on Skype, so you only need to get dressed from the waist up.

The best place for online conversation classes is italki (italki.com) Here, you can book one-on-one conversation lessons with native speakers called community tutors.

Talking to native speakers

This is, by far, the best way to learn a foreign language, but there's one problem with this method that no one talks about.

To start with, those native speakers everyone is going on about may not want to talk to you.
When you start speaking a foreign language, it's all mind blanks, silly mistakes, and sounding like a two-year-old, which makes communication slow and awkward.

It's not you that's the problem. You have to go through that stage if you want to speak a foreign language.
But you need the right people to practice with. Supportive ones who encourage you to speak and don't make you feel embarrassed when you get stuck or make mistakes.

The best place to find these people?

The internet.

The fastest (and most enjoyable way) to learn a language is with regular, one-on-one speaking practice. Online tutors are perfect because it's so easy to work with them—you can do a lesson whenever it suits you and from wherever you have an internet connection, which makes it simple to stick to regular lessons.

Let's just run through how to sign up with italki, although the procedure is much the same with other online sites:
- Go to italki.com.
- Fill in your details, including which language you're learning.

- Once you get to the main italki screen, you'll see your profile with your upcoming lessons. At the moment, it says zero, so let's go ahead and set one up.
- Click on "find a teacher."
- Here, you'll find filters like "price," "availability," and "specialties." Set these to fit in with your budget, schedule, and learning goals.
- Explore the teacher profiles and watch the introduction videos to find a teacher you'll enjoy working with.
- Click on "book now," and you'll see their lesson offers.

Informal tutoring

When choosing your lessons, you'll often see "informal tutoring," which is a pure-conversation class. This kind of lesson is great value because the tutor doesn't have to prepare anything beforehand. They just join you on Skype and start chatting

Booking your first lesson

Once you've chosen the kind of lesson you'd like, choose the time that suits you, and voilà, you've just booked your first lesson with an online tutor! Well done—I know it can feel a little intimidating at first, but creating opportunities to practice is the most important thing you can do if you want to learn to speak Portuguese. Remember: practice, practice, practice. Have I stressed that enough?

The difference between professional tutors and community tutors

When choosing a teacher, you'll also see a filter called "teacher type" and the option to choose between professional teachers and community tutors. What's the difference?

Professional teachers are qualified teachers vetted by italki—they have to upload their teaching certificate to gain this title. These classes tend to be more like "classic language lessons." The teacher will take you through a structured course, preparing lessons beforehand and teaching you new grammar and vocabulary during each lesson.

Good for:
- If you're a total beginner.
- You're not sure where to start, and you'd like guidance from an expert.

Community tutors are native speakers who offer informal tutoring, where the focus is 100% on conversation skills. They'll give you their undivided attention for an hour while you try to speak, and they'll help by giving you words and corrections you need to get your point across.

Good for:
- If you've already spent some time learning the theory and you feel like you're going round in circles. You need to put it into practice. (Remember!)
- You're happy to take control of your own learning by suggesting topics and activities you'd like to try.

- You're on a budget—these classes are usually a very good value.

If both of these options are out of your budget range, you can also use italki to find a language partner, which is free—you find a native speaker of the language you're learning (in this case, Portuguese, of course!) who also wants to learn your native language, and you teach each other. (You will find a lot of Portuguese speakers who want and are very willing to practice their English, believe me. You can also use your social media connections, that's what it's there for—socializing! Haven't got any Portuguese-speaking friends on Facebook? Make some.)

Important tip for finding the right tutor

Experiment with a few different tutors until you find one you click with. When you find a tutor you get along well with, they end up becoming like a friend—you'll look forward to meeting them and will be motivated to keep showing up to your lessons.

Prepare for your first lesson

Spending a little time preparing will allow you to focus during the lesson and get as much out of it as possible. These little gems of Portuguese can also be used to open a conversation with a native Portuguese speaker in any real-life situation, not just chatting online

Learn the basic pleasantries

"Hello," "goodbye," "please," "sorry," and "thank you" will take you a long way!

Learn basic communication phrases

It's important to try and speak in the language as much as possible without switching back into English. Those moments when you're scrambling for words and it feels like your brain's exploding—that's when you learn the most!

Whether your focus is on European or Brazilian Portuguese, fine-tuning your essentials will make life that much easier.

Here are some phrases to get you going (if you are not sure about pronunciation go to the chapter on travel):

Basic Portuguese Greetings

Greetings are often the first thing you cover when learning a new language—and in Portuguese, it's no different.

Whether you need a reminder of your basic hellos and goodbyes, or you're yet to learn them, here are some of the key greetings you need to know:

Bom dia/Boa tarde/Boa noite — Good morning/afternoon/night

Olá — Hello

Alô/Está lá — Hello (on the phone)

Note: The former is used in Brazil while you'd say the latter in Portugal.

Tchau — Bye

Até logo! — See you later!

Até amanhã — See you tomorrow

Adeus — Goodbye (formal)

Tudo bem? — How are you?

Como vai? — How's it going?

Eu estou bem, e você/e tú? — I'm good, how are you?

Note: *e você?* is the form of "and you?" most commonly used in Brazil. *E tú?* is the preferred form in Portugal, though you tend to hear it in certain parts of Brazil too.

Etiquette

Good manners always make a positive impression. If you're ever traveling to Brazil or Portugal, these terms will help prevent any cultural misunderstandings that might arise from basic etiquette:

Por favor — Please

In Brazil, *por favor* is also commonly used in the same way that "excuse me" is said in English when you're trying to politely grab someone's attention.

Com licença — Excuse me

Obrigado/Obrigada — Thank you

Note: *obrigado* is masculine and therefore said by men and boys; *obrigada* is the feminine counterpart that women and girls would use.

De nada — You're welcome

Desculpa/Desculpe — I'm sorry

Both are a variation of the same thing, though *desculpe* is slightly more formal.

Perdão — Forgive me/pardon me

Prazer — Nice to meet you

O senhor/a senhora — Formal way of saying "you" when addressing a man *(senhor)* or a woman *(senhora)*

For example: *O senhor/a senhora poderia me ajudar?* — Would you be able to help me?

Aiding Comprehension

There's no shame in asking for help when you need it. In fact, it's all part of the learning experience.

If you're talking to a native Portuguese speaker, use these phrases to aid your comprehension:

Você/O senhor/A senhora) Fala inglês? — Do you speak English?

In Portugal, just saying *Fala inglês?* will suffice. In Brazil, it's more common to precede with *você* or, if appropriate, the more formal versions of "you."

Alguém aqui fala inglês. — Does anyone here speak English?

Não compreendo — I don't understand

Eu compreendo — I understand

Não entendi — I didn't understand [what you said]

Entendi — I understood/I understand (the past in this sense is used as an affirmation)

Eu não sei — I don't know

Como se diz... em Português? — How do you say ... in Portuguese?

Fale mais devagar, por favor — Please speak more slowly

Getting out There

Traveling to Brazil or Portugal? Then these questions will definitely help you along the way. This is by no means a comprehensive list, but it'll help you get started:

Onde é o banheiro? — Where is the bathroom? (Brazilian Portuguese)

Onde fica a casa de banho? — Where is the bathroom? (European Portuguese)

Quanto custa? — How much does this cost?

Que horas são? — What time is it?

Que horas abre/fecha? — What time does this place open/close?

Para onde vai esse trem/ônibus? — Where does this train/bus go?

Como chego ao (à)... — How do I get to...?

Grammar note: use *ao* for masculine nouns, *à* for feminine.

For instance: *Como chego à estação de trem?* — How do I get to the train station?; *Como chego ao ponto de ônibus?* — How do I get to the bus stop?

Você pode me mostrar no mapa? — Could you show me on the map [where this is]?

Essentials

Qual é o seu nome? — What is your name?

Me chamo… — My name is…

An alternative to this is: *Meu nome é…*

Estou com saudades/Tenho saudades — I miss you (Brazilian/European Portuguese respectively)

Eu estou doente — I'm sick

Preciso de sua/tua ajuda — I need your help (Use *sua* in Brazil and *tua* in Portugal)

Sim/não — Yes/no

Quando? — When?

Por quê? — Why?

Vamos! — Let's go!

CHAPTER TWO

LEARNING PORTUGUESE ON YOUR OWN

If you want to learn Portuguese independently, you're going to need a few things in your head-locker.

- Motivation (to keep going)
- Focus/Mindfulness (to be effective)
- Time/Patience (for everything to sink in)

Without these three things, it's impossible to learn a language.

There seems to be one killer rule to set yourself up for success: **keep it simple!**

With tonnes of Portuguese websites, apps, and courses out there, it can be tempting to jump from one to the next.

But there's one golden rule to remember ...

It's usually more effective to calmly work your way through one book or stick with one study method than to try different things out of curiosity. It is therefore doubly important to pick the right study methods. The best will

be referred to in this book so you don't waste your valuable study time.

The focus you'll get from this keeps self-doubt away and helps you learn more deeply.

If you are learning by yourself, for whatever reasons, you will have to *work* a little bit every day at your Portuguese to succeed. Dedicating a regular amount of time every day, no matter how little, is more productive than learning sporadically in large chunks.

You will need to spend a lot of your time listening to Portuguese. If you don't, how do you expect to ever be able to follow along in a conversation?

If you are completely new to studying and like to read, then there is a pretty neat way of starting off your Portuguese adventure with an online program called: *Portuguese Uncovered* (https://www.iwillteachyoualanguage.com/portuguese-courses).

In *Portuguese Uncovered*, you learn through story. The story (a kind of mystery) is told over 20 chapters. The course is structured so that each teaching module is based on one chapter of the story.

It is not structured like a normal Portuguese course because the course syllabus emerges from the story.

It works like this:

Most Portuguese courses are structured by taking a bunch of grammar rules, putting them together in a certain order, and then teaching them to you one-by-one in a series of lessons.

This is dull; it smacks of dusty old classrooms and the droning of boring and repetitive lessons and consequently, it is ineffective.

Portuguese Uncovered is different because your main focus is to just read and enjoy the story!

And that's why it works.

You concentrate on reading and understanding the story. The *formal study* happens another way!

This is a process known as *guided discovery*.

So what is guided discovery?

Well, rather than teaching you a particular grammar rule in an abstract way, you first see the grammar rule being used in the story itself - in context - so you get to learn how it works in a natural way.

This means the course syllabus emerges from the story. (Doesn't that sound more exciting than *normal* textbooks?)

You discover the rules by yourself (with help from the story), which makes learning much more effective.

This means you get to enjoy learning Portuguese first and foremost rather than get bogged down in technicalities from the start. It's a fun way to begin your Portuguese learning experience.

Self-study and online learning are the most flexible ways to learn anything as you can base your learning around your lifestyle rather than working to the schedule of a rigid language school. By being able to work on your Portuguese in your lunch break, on your commute, in a cafe, or at home, you have the flexibility to learn at your speed, making it much easier to be successful.

CHAPTER THREE

PRACTICING PORTUGUESE ON YOUR OWN

It is very important to regularly practice the Portuguese you have learned even if it is just talking out loud to yourself. To really succeed in Portuguese (become fluent), it is essential to practice with a native speaker, but until you have found someone to practice with, here are some ways to practice by yourself.

Think in Portuguese

One of the main things about learning to speak a language is that you always have to learn to think in the language.

If you're always thinking in English when you speak Portuguese, you need to translate everything in your head while you speak. That's not easy and takes time.

It doesn't matter how fluent your Portuguese is; it's always hard to switch between two languages in your mind.

That's why you need to start thinking in Portuguese as well as speaking it. You can do this during your daily life.

If you discover a new word in Portuguese, reach for your Portuguese dictionary rather than your Portuguese-to-English dictionary. (Don't have dictionaries?—Buy some. You will need them; they can be your best friends while learning Portuguese.)

Think out loud

Now that you're already thinking in Portuguese—why don't you think out loud?

Talking to yourself whenever you're on your **own** (in case people think you are going insane) is a great way to improve your language-speaking skills.

When you're reading books in Portuguese, try doing it out loud, too.

The problem with speaking on your own is when you make mistakes. There's nobody there to correct you.

However, it's helpful to improve your ability to speak out loud, even if you make the occasional error.

Talk to the mirror

Stand in front of a mirror and talk in Portuguese.

You could pick a topic to talk about and time yourself.

Can you talk about soccer for two minutes? Can you explain what happened in the news today for three minutes?

While you're talking, you need to watch the movements of your mouth and body.

Don't allow yourself to stop. If you can't remember the particular word, then you need to express the same thing with different words.

After a couple of minutes, it's time to look up any words you didn't know. This will allow you to discover which words and topics you need to work to improve.

Fluency over grammar

The most important thing when speaking isn't grammar; **it's fluency.**

You don't want to be stopping and starting all the time. You need to be able to have free-flowing conversations with native speakers.

Don't allow yourself to stop and stumble over phrases. A minor error here and there doesn't matter.

You need to make yourself understood rather than focus on everything being perfect.

Try some travalinguas (tongue-twisters)

"Travalinguas" is the Portuguese word for tongue-twisters. "Trava" means to make mistakes, while "lingua" means tongue/language.

This includes words or phrases that are difficult to say at speed. Try out these Portuguese tongue-twisters:

O doce respondeu pro doce que o doce mais doce era o doce de batata doce.

The sweet answered the sweet that the sweeter sweet was the sweet potato sweet.

Sabia que o sabiá sabia assobiar?

Did you know that the thrush could whistle?

O rato roeu a roupa do rei de Roma.

The rat nibbled the King of Rome's clothes.

O rato roeu a rolha da garrafa de rum do rei da Rússia.

The rat nibbled the cork of the bottle of rum of the king of Russia.

Um prato de trigo para três tigres.

One dish of wheat to three tigers

Três tristes tigres.

Three sad tigers

Um sábio soube saber que o sabiá sabia assobiar.

A wise man knew to know that a bird knew to whistle.

Xico xereta chupava chupeta chutou a caixinha puxou a gaveta.

Curious Xico sucked the pacifier, kicked the box pulled the shelf.

If you can master tongue-twisters in Portuguese, you'll find that you'll improve your overall ability to pronounce challenging words in Portuguese.

Listen and repeat over and over

Check out Portuguese-language TV shows or movies to improve your Portuguese (there is a chapter dedicated to this later on).

Listen carefully and, then pause and repeat. You can attempt to replicate the accent of the person on the screen.

If you need some help to understand the meaning, turn on subtitles for extra help. If you come across a word you don't recognize, you can look it up in your Portuguese dictionary.

Learn some Portuguese songs

If you want a really fun way to learn a language, you can learn the lyrics to your favorite songs.

You can start with children's song and work yourself up to the classics.
And if you want a greater challenge, check out the Portuguese rappers. If you can keep up the pace with some of these hip-hop artists, you're doing great!

Learn phrases and common sayings

Instead of concentrating on learning new words—why not try to learn phrases and common sayings?

You can boost your vocabulary and learn how to arrange the words in a sentence like a native speaker.

You need to look out for how native speakers express stuff. You can learn a lot from listening to others.

Imagine different scenarios

Sometimes, you can imagine different scenarios in which you have to talk about different kinds of things.

For example, you can pretend to be in an interview for a job in a Portuguese-speaking country.

You can answer questions such as: "What are your biggest weaknesses?" and "Why do you want to work for us?"

When you have already prepared for such circumstances, you'll know what to say when the time comes.

Change the language on your devices

Consider changing your phone, computer, tablet, Facebook page, and anything else with a language option to Portuguese. This is an easy way to practice Portuguese since you'll see more of the vocabulary on a daily basis.

For example, every time you look at your phone, you'll see the date in Portuguese, reinforcing the days of the week and months of the year. Facebook will ask you if you would like to *adicionar amigos*, teaching you the verb that means "to add."

Seeing a few of the same words over and over again will help the language feel more natural to you, and you'll find it becomes easier to incorporate them into everyday life with very little effort involved!

Research in Portuguese

How many times a day do you Google something that you're curious about? If you use Wikipedia a few times a week, go for the Portuguese version of the website first. Next time you need information about your favorite celebrity, look at their page in Portuguese and see how much you can understand before switching the language to English!

Pick up a Portuguese newspaper

You can read Portuguese newspapers online. I recommend *Correjo de Manhä* (Morning Mail) which is a leading daily Portuguese-language newspaper based in Lisbon or if you are more interested in Brazilian Portuguese *O Dia* is a leading daily newspaper based in Rio de Janeiro.

You can also download apps and read the news on your phone. You can read the articles out loud to practice Portuguese pronunciation in addition to reading skills. This is also a great way to stay informed about what is happening in Portuguese-speaking countries and helps if you get in a Portuguese conversation.

Play games in Portuguese

Once your phone is in Portuguese, many of your games will appear in Portuguese, too. Trivia games force you to be quick on your feet as you practice Portuguese, as many of them are timed. If that isn't for you, WordBrain offers an interesting vocabulary challenge in Portuguese! (See the chapter on apps).

Watch TV Shows and You Tube videos

Don't knock Portuguese *telenovelas* until you try them! If you follow any British soaps, you will enjoy them. They come in two flavors: Portugal Portuguese and Brazilian Portuguese. Netflix, Amazon, Apple, Hulu and many other streaming channels now offer shows and movies in Portuguese, some of which include English subtitles so you can check how much you understand. You can also watch your favorite movies with Portuguese subtitles.

As for *telenovelas*, the better ones (in my opinion) come from Brazil. The production value is higher than in shows from most other Latin American countries, where *telenovelas* are a stable for the viewing public.

Don't have Netflix, Amazon, Apple or Hulu? Try websites such as NOS, TVI or SIC. If you don't wish to pay for any of these there is always YouTube. You can also check out free Portuguese lessons on YouTube in your spare time. This is a good way to judge the stage your Portuguese learning has reached. If you are a beginner, look for lessons that teach you how to say the letters and sounds of the Portuguese alphabet. It will help with your pronunciation. (See the chapter on best Portuguese TV shows).

Get Portuguese-language music for your daily commute

Why not practice Portuguese during your commute? Singing along to songs will help your pronunciation and help you begin to think in Portuguese (not a good idea if you use public transportation unless, of course, you have a superb singing voice). Try to learn the lyrics.

You can get music in any genre in Portuguese on YouTube, just like in English. If you like soft rock, I suggest Filipe Sambado, Lince, Madrepaz, Prana, Surma and Ermo.

If you can keep up with Portuguese and Brazilian rappers then you really will be on your way to becoming fluent.

Portuguese hip-hop's trajectory (or Rap Tuga, as fans call it) is in many ways an ultra-condensed version of *fado's* path. (which many argue originates from Brazil and is a direct result of colonialism) and *Cante Alentejano,* they have both been classified as Intangible Cultural Heritage by UNESCO. What was once a marginal genre of social protest confined mostly to the outskirts of Chelas, the Linha de Sintra, and the Margem Sul do Tejo is now eminently profitable.

Let's look at some of the most prominent Portuguese rappers you should know:

- **Allen Halloween.** There's a phrase in Portuguese that goes, "Primeiro estranha-se, depois entranha-se." It is notoriously difficult to translate into English. I'd go for, "First you find it weird, then you get it." This phrase came to mind after hearing Allen Halloween's voice for the first time.
- **Slow J**. Since his 2015 debut EP *The Free Food Tape*, Slow J has quietly become one of the most talented all-around musical acts in Portugal. Rapper, singer, and producer, "You Are Forgiven" is, considered one of the best Rap Tuga albums of 2019.
- **Papillon.** Papillon got his start with the rap group GROGnation, but since the release of his 2018 album *Deepak Looper* (produced by none other than the multitalented Slow J), he has emerged as one of the Rap Tuga's most promising names. The story behind

Deepak Looper is a bit of a rap fairy tale — Slow J was asked in an interview what rappers he would most like to work with, and Papillon was at the top of the list.

- **Wet Bed Gang.** Wet Bed Gang is a perpetual finalist for the worst rap moniker of all time, but the group's place as Portugal's foremost pop-rap group is undeniable. In their latest single "iNrresponsável" (a pun on the word "irresponsible"), they follow in the footsteps of trailblazers Johnny Knoxville, Uncle Drew, and Freddie Gibbs.
- **Nenny.** To speak of Nenny's discography would be a contradiction in terms — we are forced instead to talk about her number of songs available to the public, which you can count on one hand. Despite only having released a few songs to date, Nenny has left me no choice but to include her on this list. She is, as Ricardo Farinha notes, the first truly viral woman rapper in the history of Portuguese hip-hop.

Brazilian rap has always felt caught between two worlds, unsure of whether to experiment with music indigenous to the country or follow the trusted pattern of American boom-bap. Cultural proximity to the US (namely in places like Miami and Boston, both of which have large Brazilian populations) has always guaranteed a link between the two country's musical outputs; it's often unclear who is emulating whom.

Let's look at some of the most prominent Brazilian rappers you should know:

- **Rincon Sapiência**. Rincon Sapiência is Brazil's great crossover rapper loved by purists, trapheads, and casual listeners alike. While recent BR rap has turned away from its big brother in Brazilian funk and veered toward trap, Sapiência is unique in that he manages to incorporate both into his music — in most of his popular hits, you can hear the *tamborzão* beat that makes Brazilian funk so distinctive. Sapiência's wide appeal, however, doesn't prevent him from writing unapologetically and directly about racial injustice in Brazil.
- **Baco Exu do Blues**. Northeastern Bahía native Baco Exu do Blues caught fire in 2016 with his song "Sulicídio," (a pun that amounts to something like "Southicide"), in which he criticizes Brazilian rap for being so São Paulo and Rio-centric. Since then, Baco has released a string of R&B-inspired love songs with singers like Tuyo and 1LUM3 that have garnered more than 20 million streams and have found a larger audience outside of hardcore rap heads.
- **Djonga**. Born in the Índio favela of Belo Horizonte, Djonga is the latest reminder that being from São Paulo or Rio is no longer a prerequisite for making it as a rapper. For the last three years (on every March 14), Djonga has released a new album. With an aggressive flow, provocative music videos, and subject matter mostly about Brazil's dramatic racial inequality, Djonga has the attention of all of Brazilian rap in a vice grip. His videos are at once imaginative and utterly necessary.

- **Young Buda**. On any given Yung Buda song, there will be, at least, three languages – Japanese, English, and Portuguese. In his three releases, all EP's of around 14-15 minutes, Buda has perfected the sort of mid 2000s technobliss that Swedish former wunderkind Yung Lean more or less invented in his earliest releases. The music video for "Autumn Ring Mini," whose title is a reference to the *Gran Turismo* video game series, is a beautiful, perfect summation of everything Buda — streetcar culture, anime, trap, and art escapism. In the song, Buda also references Amaterasu who, besides being a Shinto sun goddess, is also the protagonist of an obscure but critically acclaimed PS2 game called *Ōkami*.
- **CHS**. CHS probably won't win any awards for reinventing the rap game, but since his days with the rap group Nectar Gang, he has put out an incredibly consistent body of music. He has a knack for creative hooks that are impossible to forget. It was with Nectar Gang that CHS earned a place in Brazilian rap, but as the group's various members have focused on their respective solo careers, CHS has taken off since the release of his debut album *CHAOS*.

Listen to podcasts in Portuguese

While you're sitting at your desk, driving in your car on your way to work, or cooking dinner at home, put on a podcast in Portuguese. It could be one aimed at teaching Portuguese or a Portuguese-language podcast on another topic.

For learning conversational Portuguese, try Coffee Break Portuguese, (https://radiolingua.com/2009/05/lesson-01-one-minute-portuguese/), which focuses on conversations for traveling abroad, like how to order coffee! If you are a true beginner, PortuguesePod101 (https://www.portuguesepod101.com/) is another great one. They have all levels of Portuguese for any student!

Duolingo (https://www.duolingo.com/) has also just added a great new feature called "stories": fun, simple tales for learners with interactive translations and mini comprehension quizzes.

CHAPTER FOUR

A GUIDE FOR THE COMPLETE BEGINNER

If you are a complete beginner, you can consider using this book as a guide on *how* to learn and *what* to learn to enable you to speak Portuguese as painlessly as possible. This guide will hand over the keys to learning Portuguese for any and all potential learners, but in particular, it is for those who think they might face more trouble than most. It'll be more than enough to get you up and running.

These are the main subjects we will be covering as you begin to learn *how to learn* Portuguese. You will probably notice that I repeat the idea of motivation throughout this book. That is because it is important. It is one of the main reasons people fail to achieve their goal of speaking Portuguese and give up before they really get started:

- **Motivation:** Defining your overarching goal
- **Step by Step:** Setting achievable short-term goals

- **Getting There:** Efficient Portuguese learning resources for beginners
- **Fun:** Having fun as you learn
- **Ongoing Motivation:** Staying motivated as you learn

We will go over each of these subjects in more detail later, but for now, below is a brief overview.

Definition of Motivation: a reason or reasons for acting or behaving in a particular way.

Motivation is critical for learning a language. Good, motivating reasons for learning Portuguese include:

- "I want to understand people at samba events."
- "I want to flirt with that cute Portuguese/Brazilian person at work."
- "I want to read José Saramago in the original."
- "I want to understand people at my local Portuguese/Brazilian restaurant."
- "I want to enjoy *telenovelas* (Portuguese and Brazilian soap operas—more on these later)."
- "I need Portuguese for work so that I can communicate with clients."
- "I want to be able to make myself understood when I'm on holiday in Portugal or Brazil."

These are all great reasons for learning Portuguese because they include **personal, compelling motivations** that'll keep you coming back when the going gets rough.

They also guide you to **specific, achievable goals** for study (more on this later), like focusing on reading or on the vocabulary used in conversations on the dance floor.

Here are a few bad—but rather common—reasons for studying Portuguese:

- "I want to tell people I speak Portuguese."
- "I want to have Portuguese on my CV."
- "I want to look smart."

Why are these bad?:

These are very likely not going to be truly motivating reasons when you can't seem to find time to open that workbook. They also don't give you any concrete desire to pay careful attention to, for example, a new tense that you've come across and how it might allow you to express yourself better.

If looking smart is your honest reason for wanting to learn a language, perhaps you could just lie and say you speak something like Quechua, which few people are going to be able to call you out on. (If you are interested, Quechua was the ancient language of the Incas and is still spoken in remote parts of South America).

Learning a language is a serious commitment

It is rarely possible to learn a language without a genuine motivation for some sort of authentic communication. That does not mean it should be painful or boring. Throughout this book, I will outline methods that make learning Portuguese fun and interesting. When you are interested in something and having fun you do not have to consciously **TRY**, and strangely, this is when you perform at your best. You are in the *zone,* as they say.

Step by Step: Setting achievable, short-term goals.

As in life, once you are clear about your overall motivation(s), these should then be translated into achievable, short-term goals.

You're not going to immediately get every joke passed around at the local Portuguese/Brazilian bar and be able to respond in kind, but you should be able to more quickly arrive at goals like:

- "I'm going to place my favorite restaurant order in perfect Portuguese." We go over this in the chapter entitled "Navigating the restaurant."
- "I'm going to memorize *and use* three words of Portuguese and Brazilian slang." We go over this in the chapter entitled "Partying in Brazil or Portugal."

First of all, though, we have to get something out of the way (remember, you can skip this and come back to it later or ignore it completely if it does not apply or you find it boring—in fact, you can do this with any of the chapters).

Differences between Brazil Portuguese and Portugal Portuguese

There are varieties of Portuguese spoken throughout Brazil America and in Portugal itself. Of course, a native speaker will understand all of them, but for a new learner, it might seem confusing. So, what are the real differences between Brazil Portuguese and Portugal Portuguese?

Surprisingly Portuguese is one of the world's most widely spoken languages, placing sixth behind Chinese, Spanish, English, Hindi, and Arabic. There are two main kinds of Portuguese: Brazilian (spoken in Brazil) and European (spoken in many countries in Europe, including Portugal). While they have some similarities, there are certainly many differences in intonation, pronunciation, grammar and vocabulary.

In general, those who speak either language can understand the other, but it may be difficult in some situations. That's because there are so many nuances between the two. American linguist Albert Marckwardt coined the term "Colonial Lag" as a hypothesis that original varieties of a language (i.e., Brazilian Portuguese) change less than the variety spoken in the mother country (Portugal). This also happens with Spanish spoken in Spain and that in Latin America.

Why did and does this happen?

Countries tend to follow the linguistic developments of the mother country with a bit of delay due to the geographical distance. Portuguese was not deemed the official language in

Brazil until 1758, whereas the colonization really began in the 16th century. Over time, changes occurred in the language because of increasing contact with European and Asian immigrants.

The other countries colonized by Portugal speak a Portuguese more akin to the mother language. Why? Many of them are African countries, so they don't have external contact from other cultures that could have impacted their way of speaking. Secondly, compared to Brazil, those countries gained their independence much later and had more contact with Portugal during their early development.

The differences in pronunciation

Pronunciation is one of the main differences between the languages. Brazilians speak vowels longer and wider, while Portuguese pronounce the words with a more closed mouth, without pronouncing the vowels as much.

The pronunciation of some consonants is also different, particularly the S at the end of a word. In Brazilian Portuguese, an S at the end of a word is pronounced as SS; in Portugal, it is pronounced as SH.

Accents

Brazilian Portuguese is thought to be more phonetically pleasing to the ear thanks to its open vowels, while European Portuguese can sound somewhat garbled. Brazilian accents have a strong cadence and lift to them, making it easier to learn and understand.

Grammar and Spelling

Some words are spelled differently. For instance, reception in European Portuguese is "receção", but in Brazilian Portuguese there is an audible p to the spelling of "recepção." In other words, the letter p is audible in Brazilian Portuguese and silent in European Portuguese.

Brazilians are more creative with their use of Portuguese, converting some nouns into verbs. To congratulate uses the Portuguese phrase — "dar os parabéns" — but Brazilians may condense the expression into one verb – "parabenizar."

Sometimes, Brazilian Portuguese takes words from American English, ignoring its Latin roots. European Portuguese usually adopts words from Latin roots, keeping the original spelling. Overall, European Portuguese is more resistant to change and assimilation of foreign words.

Formal and informal speech

European Portuguese is the more formal of the two versions. In Brazilian Portuguese, the word **você** is used for "you" in informal settings; in European Portuguese, **tu** is utilized in the same context. In Portugal, they view the você as crude and thus remove the second-person pronoun in less casual situations and instead use the verb in the third-person singular. When describing actions, Brazilians use "estou fazendo" to

mean "I am doing," and the European Portuguese use the infinitive form, "estou a fazer." The latter is less direct and translates to "I am taken to doing."
Should you learn Brazilian or European Portuguese?

This is a highly personal decision. This will depend on your personal motives, availability of resources, future aspirations and goals. In general, the thing that sparked your interest in the language will have a direct impact on the dialect you choose. For example, if you love classic literature, European Portuguese might be the best way to go for you. If you love Carnival and samba, Brazilian Portuguese may be best.

The availability of resources will also influence your decision. *"Brazil has a larger population than Portugal with many native speakers, impacting* availability *of content. In other words, it's simpler to locate resources for Brazilian Portuguese learners than it is for those who study the European kind"* says Ryan McMunn of BRIC Language Systems. Finding a professional resource that offers instruction in Brazilian Portuguese with access to native speakers will greatly improve your chances of being successful and learning both at your pace and in a way that will last.

Future goals

What are your future plans? The answer will help you determine which Portuguese variety would be best for you. If you would like to work for the United Nations someday, you should learn Continental Portuguese because its operations are based in Europe. If you want a job in a North American enterprise, Brazilian Portuguese will be best because that country has a bigger economic and trading base.

Still can't decide between the two?

If you are still unable to decide which option makes the most sense for you to pursue, here are a few factors to consider:

You may want to go with European Portuguese if you:

- Want to travel, live in or work in Portugal.
- Want to access a wider spectrum of Portuguese-speaking countries (most of them are more aligned with the European accent).
- Want to learn a more formal and traditional version of the language.
- Are drawn to the European experience, from its ancient history to its Mediterranean lifestyle

Consider learning Brazilian Portuguese if you:

- Wish to travel, live in or work in Brazil.
- Want an easier, more informal version of the language to learn.
- Want to apply your linguistic skills to break into a bigger economic market.
- Love Latin American cultures and traditions.

Portuguese, both Brazilian and European, is a beautiful and romantic language. While the style you learn will be catered by your surroundings and interests, the beauty of the language will remain and will be one you can enjoy for years to come.

I cannot stress enough the importance of correct pronunciation, as this will form the basis of your learning experience. There are a lot of free online pronunciation guides, make the most of them. It is also a good idea, if you have the equipment to record yourself and compare it to the native speaker.

Talk when you read or write in Portuguese. *Writing* itself is an important part of language learning so read out loud (paying careful attention to pronunciation) and write in Portuguese as much as you can. Just like when you took notes at school, writing serves to reinforce your learning.

- Watch movies with subtitles. Imitate some of the characters if you want.
- Listen to Portuguese music, learn the lyrics of your favorite songs, and sing along with them.
- Join a local Portuguese/Brazilian social group. You'd be surprised how many there are and how helpful they can be for new language learners. This will give you a chance to practice your Portuguese with a native speaker in a friendly and helpful environment.

CHAPTER FIVE

FLUENCY

What is fluency? Every person has a different answer to that question. The term is imprecise, and it means a little less every time someone writes another book, article, or spam email with a title like "U can B fluent in 7 days!"

A lot of people are under the impression that to be fluent in another language means to speak it as well as, or almost as well as, your native language. These people define fluency as knowing a language *perfectly*—lexically, grammatically and even phonetically. If that is the case, then I very much doubt that there are that many fluent English speakers out there. By that, I mean that they know every aspect of English grammar and know every word in the English language.

I prefer to define it as "being able to speak and write quickly or easily in a given language." It comes from the Latin word *fluentum,* meaning "to flow."

There is also a difference between translating and interpreting, though they are often confused. The easiest way to remember the difference is that translating deals with the written word while interpreting deals with the spoken word. I suppose, to be pedantic, one should be fluent in both forms, but for most people, when they think of fluency, they mean the spoken word. Nobody has ever asked me to write them something in Spanish, for example, but I am quite often asked to say something in Spanish, as though this somehow proves my fluency—which is a bit weird when you think about it as it is only people who have no knowledge of Spanish whatsoever who ask me that and I could say any old nonsense and they would believe it was Spanish.

The next question most people ask is: how long does it take to be fluent? It is different for every person. But let's use an example to make a baseline calculation. To estimate the time you'll need, you need to consider your fluency goals, the language(s) you already know, the language you're learning, and your daily time constraints.

One language is not any more difficult to learn than another; it just depends on how difficult it is for *you* to learn. For example, Japanese may be difficult to learn for many English speakers for the same reason that English is difficult for many Japanese speakers; there are very few words and grammar concepts that overlap, plus an entirely different alphabet. In contrast, an English speaker learning French has much less work to do. English vocabulary is 28% French and 28% Latin, so as soon as an English speaker learns French pronunciation, they already know thousands of words. If you want to check the approximate difficulty of learning a new language for an English speaker, you can check with the US Foreign Service Institute, which grades them by "class hours needed to learn."

CHAPTER SIX

FORGETTING

We struggle to reach any degree of fluency because there is so much to remember. The rulebook of the language game is too long. We go to classes that discuss the rulebook, and we run drills about one rule or another, but we never get to play the game (actually put our new found language to use). On the off chance that we ever reach the end of a rulebook, we've forgotten most of the beginning already. Moreover, we've ignored the *other* book (the vocabulary book), which is full of thousands upon thousands of words that are just as hard to remember as the rules.

Forgetting is the greatest foe, so we need a plan to defeat it. What's the classic Portuguese-language-learning success story? A guy moves to Brazil, falls in love with a Brazilian girl (not difficult), and spends every waking hour practicing the language until he is fluent within the year. This is the immersion experience, and it defeats forgetting with brute force. In large part, the proud, Portuguese-speaking hero is successful because he never had any time to forget. Every day, he swims in an ocean of Portuguese; how could he forget what he has learned?

Immersion is a wonderful experience, but if you have steady work, a dog, a family, or a bank account in need of refilling, you can't readily drop everything and devote *that* much of your life to learning a language. We need a more practical way to get the right information into our heads and prevent it from leaking out of our ears.

I'm going to show you how to stop forgetting so you can get to the actual game. The important thing to know is what to remember so that once you start playing the game, you're good at it. Along the way, you will rewire your ears to hear new sounds and rewire your tongue to master a new accent. You will investigate the makeup of words, how grammar assembles those words into thoughts, and how to make those thoughts come out of your mouth without needing to waste time translating. You'll learn to make the most of your limited time, investigating which words to learn first, how to use mnemonics to memorize abstract concepts faster, and how to improve your reading, writing, listening, and speaking skills as quickly and effectively as possible.

It is just as important to understand how to use these tools as it is to understand *why* they work. Language learning is one of the most intensely personal journeys you can ever undertake. You are going into your own mind and altering the way you think.

- Make memories more memorable.
- Maximize laziness.
- Don't review. Recall.
- Rewrite the past.

How to remember a Portuguese word forever

You can consider this part of the book to be a miniature mental time machine. It will take you back to the time when you learned as a child does.

Kids have amazing brains. They can pick up two languages in early childhood just as easily as they can learn one. Early childhood also seems to be the key period when musical training makes it much easier to acquire the skill known as perfect or absolute pitch. And that's not all: kids and teens can learn certain skills and abilities much more quickly than most adults. In a way, it makes sense that the young brain is so "plastic," or able to be molded. When we're young and learning how to navigate the world, we need to be able to acquire skills and knowledge fast.

As we age, we lose much of that plasticity. Our brains and personalities become more "set," and certain things are harder to learn or change.

As adults in the rapidly changing modern world, where the ability to learn a new skill is perhaps more essential than ever, it's easy to be jealous of how quickly kids can pick up on things.

How does one go from being a baby, whose linguistic skills end with smiling, burping, and biting, to being a fluent speaker whose English is marked by appropriate diction, golden grammar, and a killer accent?

Normal, everyday children do this in about 20 months.

This brings us back to the question: how do children learn a language? And what lessons can foreign-language learners get from these precious children?

So, we're going to trace a baby's journey from babbling newborn to kindergartner. Along the way, we'll note the milestones of language development

Pre-birth

We used to think that language learning began at the moment of birth. But scientists in Washington, Stockholm, and Helsinki discovered that fetuses are actually listening inside the womb.

They gave mothers a recording of made-up words to play during the final weeks of pregnancy. The babies heard the pseudo-words around 50—71 times while inside their mother's womb. After they were born, these babies were tested. By hooking them up to an EEG, scientists were able to see images of the babies' brains when the made-up words were played.

To their astonishment, the babies remembered and recognized the words that were presented when they were in the womb.

You know what this suggests, right?

It points to prenatal language learning.

It turns out, the first day of learning language isn't when one is born, but 30 weeks into the pregnancy when babies start to develop their hearing ability. So, be careful what you say around a pregnant woman, ok? Somebody's listening.

0—6 Months

Newborn babies are keen listeners in their environments. They particularly like to listen to the voice of their mother, and they quickly differentiate it from other voices. They also learn to recognize the sounds of her language from a foreign one.

Baby communication centers on expressing pain and pleasure. And if you listen very carefully, you'll notice that babies have different types of cries for different needs. A cry for milk is different from a cry for a new diaper—although a flustered first-time father might not hear any difference.

Around the fourth month, babies engage in "vocal play" and babble unintelligible sounds—including those that begin with the letters M, P, and B. (This is when mommy swears that she heard baby say, "Mama.")

6—12 Months.

This is the peek-a-boo stage.

Babies pay attention and smile when you call them by name.

They also start responding to "Hi!" and "Good morning."

At this stage, babies continue babbling and having fun with language. But this time, their unintelligible expressions have put on a certain kind of sophistication. They seem to be putting words together. You could've sworn she was telling you something.

It will actually be around this time when babies learn their first words ("no," "mama," "dada," and so on).

By the 12th month, you'll have that nagging feeling that she understands more than she lets on. And you will be right. Babies, although they can't speak much, recognize a lot. They begin to recognize keywords like "cup," "ball," "dog," and "car."

And on her first birthday, she'll definitely learn what the word "cake" means.

1—2 Years Old.

This is the "Where's-your-nose?" stage.

Babies learn to differentiate and point to the different parts of their bodies. They're also very receptive to queries like "Where's Daddy?" and requests like "Clap your hands" or "Give me the book."

As always, her comprehension goes ahead of her ability to speak. But in this stage, she'll be learning even more words. Her utterances will graduate into word pairs like "eat cake," "more play," and "no ball."

This is also the time when she loves hearing those sing-along songs and rhymes. And guess what? She'll never tire of these, so be prepared to listen to her favorite rhymes over and over and over again.

2—4 Years Old.

There will be a tremendous increase in learned words at this stage. She now seems to have a name for everything—from the cups she uses to her shoes and toys. She gains more nouns, verbs, and adjectives in her linguistic arsenal.

Her language structure becomes more and more complicated. Her sentences get longer, and her grammar mistakes get slowly weeded out. This time, she can express statements like "I'm hungry, Mommy" or "My friend gave me this."

She'll start to get really talkative and ask questions like, "Where are we going, Daddy?"

By this time, you'll begin to suspect that she's preparing to ask ever more difficult questions.

The child has learned the language and has become a native speaker.

So, what are the lessons we can take away from children as foreign-language learners?

We've just gone over how babies progress to acquire their first language.

Is there something in this process that adult language learners can emulate in their quest to learn foreign languages? Well, as it turns out, there is.

Understanding this early childhood learning process has major implications for adult language learners.

In this chapter, we're going to peek behind the curtain and look even deeper into how children learn languages to reap four vital lessons.

Each one of these lessons is an essential part of linguistic success.

1. The Centrality of Listening.

We learned in the previous section that listening comes very early in the language-acquisition process. Babies get a masterclass on the different tones, rhythms and sounds of a language even before they see the light of day.

Without listening, they'd have no building blocks from which to build their own repertoire of sounds.

Listening is so important for language acquisition that babies don't fully develop their language capabilities without the ability to hear. Thus, we have the deaf-mute pairing. How can one learn to speak when one can't even hear others or oneself doing it?

In addition, children who suffer hearing problems early in life experience delays in their expressive and receptive communication skills. Their vocabulary develops slower, and they often have difficulty understanding abstract words (e.g., extreme, eager, and pointless). Their sentences are also shorter and simpler.

In general, the greater the hearing loss, the poorer the children do in academic evaluations.

Listening is central to language.

It's the first language skill humans develop.

And yet, how many language programs pound on the issue of listening as a central skill, as opposed to grammar or vocabulary?

Listening is deceptive, isn't it? It seems like nothing's happening. It's too passive an activity, unlike speaking. When speaking, you actually hear what was learned. The benefits of listening are initially unheard (pun intended).

Contrary to common belief, listening can be an intensely active activity.

So, as a foreign-language learner, you need to devote time to actively listening to your target language. Don't just play those podcasts passively in the background. Actively engage in the material. If at all possible, don't multitask. Sit down and don't move—like a baby who hasn't learned how to walk.

Take every opportunity to listen to the language as spoken by native speakers. When you watch a movie or a language learning video, for example, don't just focus on the visual stimulation. Listen for the inflections, tones, and rhythms of words.

It may not look like much, but, yes, listening is that powerful.

2. The Primacy of Making Mistakes

Listening to a one-year-old talk is such a delight. They're so cute and innocent. Their initial statements betray a string of misappropriated vocabulary, fuzzy logic, and grammar violations.

When a 1-year-old points to a dog and says, "Meow," we find it so cute. When his older sister says, "I goed there today," we don't condemn the child. Instead, we correct her by gently saying, "No, Sally, not goed. Went!"

We aren't as kind to adults. We're even worse to ourselves.

Ever since we learned in school that making mistakes means lower test scores, we've dreaded making them. Mistakes? Bad. And we carry over this fear when we're learning a foreign language as adults.

That's why, unless we're 100% sure of its correctness, we don't want to blurt out a single sentence in our target language. First, we make sure that the words are in their proper order and that the verbs are in the proper tense and agree with the subject in number and gender.

Now, something tells me that a ten-month-old has no problems committing more mistakes in one sentence than she has words. In fact, she probably won't admit that there's something wrong—or ever know that something's wrong. She just goes on with her life and continues listening.

Why don't we follow this spirit of a child?

We already know that it works because the kid who once exclaimed, "My feets hurt," is now galloping towards a degree in sociology.

As a foreign-language learner, one of the things you need to make peace with is the fact that you're going to make mistakes. It comes with the territory, and you're going to have to accept that.

Make as many mistakes as you can. Make a fool out of yourself like a two-year-old and laugh along the way. Pay your dues. And if you're as diligent in correcting those mistakes as you are making them, soon enough you'll be on your way to fluency.

3. The Joy of Repetition

When your daughter is around 6-12 months old, playing peek-a-boo never gets old for her. She always registers genuine surprise every time you reveal yourself. And she'd laugh silly all day—all because of a very simple game.

And remember how, when your children were around one to two years old and they couldn't get enough of those sing-songy rhymes? They wanted you to keep pressing the "replay" button while watching their favorite cartoon musical on YouTube. You wondered when they would get sick of it.

But lo and behold, each time was like the first time. They weren't getting sick of it. In fact, it got more exciting for them.

Repetition. It's a vital element of learning. If there's one reason why babies learn so fast, it's because they learn stuff over and over—to the point of overlearning.

Adults never have the patience to overlearn a language lesson, to repeat the same lesson over and over without feeling bored to tears. Adults quickly interpret this as being "stuck". This lack of forward motion is promptly followed by the thought that time is being wasted. They think they should quickly press on to the next lesson—which they do, to the detriment of their learning.

We repeat a vocabulary word three times and expect it to stay with us for life—believing it will now be saved in our long-term memory. Quite unrealistic, isn't it?

In the prenatal experiment where made-up words were played to babies still in the womb, each word was heard by the baby at least 50 times. (Is it really a wonder, then, that the baby, when tested, recognized the words?)

Repetition is vital to learning. In fact, many apps take the concept further and introduce the idea of spaced repetition. SRS (spaced repetition software) can be an invaluable tool in your language learning toolkit. Try out Anki (https://apps.ankiweb.net/), FluentU (htttps://www.fluentu.com/), or SuperMemo (https://www.supermemo.com/en).

Unless you're a genius with an eidetic memory, repetition will be one of your most important allies in the quest for foreign-language mastery.

Repetition can take the form of replaying videos, rereading words, rewriting vocabulary, re-listening to podcasts, and re-doing games and exercises.

Keep on repeating until it becomes a habit. Because that's what a language ultimately is.

4. The Importance of Immersion

Immersion can actually push your brain to process information in the same way native speakers do.

And is there anything more immersive than a baby being born and experiencing the world by observation?

Think about what the baby is experiencing. She's like an Englishman suddenly being dropped in the middle of China without access to the internet.

Everything is new.

So, you use your innate abilities to make generalizations, read context, listen to native speakers, and imitate how they speak.

Everything is on the line. You've got to learn how to communicate fast; otherwise, you won't get to eat—even when you're sitting at a Chinese restaurant. It's a totally immersive experience where you're not learning a language just for kicks or for your resume. You're doing it for your very survival. (That takes care of the "motivation" part of your learning.)

There's nothing fake about a child learning a language. It's a totally immersive and authentic experience—all their early language lessons are learned in a meaningful social context. I have yet to meet a baby who learned his first language by enrolling in a class.

For the adult language learner, immersion can be experienced remotely. One way of achieving immersion is by getting exposed to as many language-learning videos as possible.

Another way is something we touched on earlier: **spaced repetition**.

Remember that time you crammed information for an exam?

(Don't worry, we've all been there.)

You, like many others, may have spent an all-nighter memorizing every page of your notes and trying desperately to make up for countless days you decided to hold off on studying.

While you may have performed well on the exam, think about how much you recalled a few weeks after the test date.

How much of that information did you remember?

If you're like most humans, the answer is probably not very much.

Cramming does not work, especially when learning a new language.

You can try, but unfortunately, you won't get very far if you try to learn the Portuguese subjunctive tense in one night. Now, you may wonder, "If I was able to recall information so well at the time of an exam, why has it dropped from my memory soon after?"

Well, there's science behind this! Research proves that cramming intense amounts of information into our brain in a short period is not an effective way for long-term learning.

British author H.E. Gorst mentioned in his book *The Course of Education* that cramming is what "produce[s] mediocrity". What he means is that cramming doesn't provide us with the ability to think critically and effectively apply our knowledge in creative ways.

Yet cramming is still becoming more and more popular among students of all ages.

If it's so ineffective, why do we cram?

Fingers point to improper time management as the number one cause. If we better prioritize our time, we can more efficiently learn new information. By cramming, we may absorb information that can be easily regurgitated the following day. But say goodbye to that information because it's going to disappear at an exponential rate as time goes on.

Cramming trades a strong memory now for a weak memory later. Unfortunately, we sometimes cling to short-term gratifications and fail to strive for long-term benefits. Before you banish all hope for your memory, there's an alternative method to learning that may give your brain the love it needs.

In psychology, there is a theory of memorization and learning called the "spacing effect". The spacing effect is the idea that we remember and learn items more effectively when they are studied a few times over a long span of time.

So, is frequent repetition the solution? Not quite.

Since cramming is out the window, you may think it's smarter to study material over and over again. It's crucial to note that while repetition is important, not all repetition is created equally. You'll want to space out the repetitions each time you study a set of information.

But determining how long to wait in between studying can also be a tricky matter. If you practice too soon, your brain will begin passively remembering information, which will not stick over time. If you practice too late, you will have forgotten the material and have to spend extra time relearning it. Add to this the complexity of individual learning and memorization patterns, and you have a recipe for guaranteed memory loss.

Thankfully, there is the aforementioned software available today to help us pinpoint the sweet spot of optimal learning. Just when our forgetfulness dips below a certain level, these programs jump in and keep our brains on track.

Spaced Repetition Software

Spaced repetition software (SRS) computer programs are modeled after a process similar to using flashcards. Users enter items to be memorized into the program, and they are then converted into electronic "decks" that appear on-screen in a one-by-one sequential pattern.

Usually, the user clicks one time to reveal the question or front of the generated card. A second click will reveal the answer or back of the flashcard. Upon seeing the answer, the user then indicates the difficulty of the card by telling the program how challenging it was.

Each following card's order of appearance is not random. In fact, SRS programs use algorithms to space out when each card will appear again on the screen. Cards given "easy" ratings will appear later than cards given "hard" ratings, thus allowing users to spend more time studying the cards that are more difficult. The tough ones will show up more often until they are mastered, giving you the chance to actively learn them more efficiently than with other learning styles.

Using Spaced Repetition for Language Learning

To put this into context, let's pretend you spend an evening studying a hundred Mandarin words you didn't know before. You continue studying until you've completely memorized the words. Let's say it takes you an hour to do this.

Immediately after reviewing these words, your memory of them will be quite high. However, over time, you will naturally begin forgetting the material you learned. And since it was your first time learning these words, your use-it-or-lose-it brain is more likely to ditch this new material at a faster pace. The new knowledge isn't yet considered important enough to be etched into your brain cells.

However, the second time you study the same words, it will take you less time to master the set than it did the first time. Perhaps this time it only takes you 30 minutes to memorize the hundred words. Congratulations! You've completed your first spaced repetition.

So, does this mean you'll have to keep repeating the information you want to learn for the rest of your life? Not exactly. While it does require long-term review to keep information fresh on our minds, the time spent on review becomes shorter and less frequent over time.

With each successive review, it will take you less and less time to fully recall the information. As you begin mastering a set of words, you'll find yourself whizzing through each card. Eventually, information will become so memorable that you know it by heart. This is when you know you're ready to move onto a new, more challenging deck.

Self-discipline Ultimately Trumps All

Remember, while these programs may have wonderful language-learning techniques, they won't be effective unless you have the self-discipline to use them on an ongoing basis. If you're still at a loss for where to begin with organizing your own flashcards, check out Olly Richards's "Make Words Stick", a guide for language learners just like you looking to get more out of their SRS.

Make it a habit to open up and use the software mentioned above. If you set aside some time every day to do your SRS studying, you'll see noticeable results sooner than you might imagine.

If, like me, you sometimes want to get away from the computer and get back to basics, you can make your own flashcards and use them manually. You can buy packets of blank cards at the post office or at any stationery suppliers. Write the English word on one side and the Portuguese word on the reverse. You can choose your own words, but here are 100 to get you started. If you want to know how to pronounce them (this is absolutely essential unless you are already acquainted with Portuguese pronunciation), head on over here: https://www.portuguesepod101.com/portuguese-word-lists/

semana	week
há sete dias em uma semana	there are seven days in a week.
ano	year
um ano	one year
hoje	today
hoje às seis e quinze	today at 6:15
amanhã	tomorrow
amanhã às dez e dez	tomorrow at 10:10
ontem	yesterday
calendário	calendar
um calendário anual	one calendar year
segundo	second
hora	o'clock
relógio	clock
o relógio marca oito minutos para as doze	the clock reads eight minutes to twelve

| poder | can |
| ele pode dirigir, mas não muito bem | he can drive, but not very well |

| usar | use |
| a programadora usa o computador | the programmer uses the computer |

| fazer | do |
| a mulher faz os serviços domésticos | the woman does housework |

| ir | go |
| ir reto | go straight ahead |

| vir | come |
| a menina veio em direção à filmadora | the girl came towards the video camera |

| rir | laugh |
| o casal ri de uma piada | the couple laughs at a joke |

| fazer | make |
| o chef faz suco de laranja | the chef makes orange juice |

| ver | see |
| os turistas viram o pôr-do-sol | the tourists saw the sunset |

longe	far
a mulher está olhando para alguma coisa lá longe	the woman is looking at something far away
pequeno	small
bom	good
verduras são boas para você	vegetables are good for you
bonito	beautiful
a paisagem é bonita	the scenary is beautiful
feio	ugly
cara feia	ugly face
difícil	difficult
Inglês é difícil	English is difficult
fácil	easy
mau	bad
o homem é mau	the man is bad
perto	near
Eu moro perto da universidade	I live near the university

prazer em conhecê-lo	nice to meet you
olá	hello
bom dia	good morning
boa tarde	good afternoon
boa noite	good evening/good night
tudo bem?	how are you?
obrigado	than you
não	no
delicioso!	delicious!
eu sou...	I'm... (name)
adeus	goodbye
sim	yes
segunda-feira	Monday
terça-feira	Tuesday
quarta-feira	Wednesday
quinta-feira	Thursday
sexta-feira	Friday
sábado	Saturday

domingo	Sunday
domingo, dia dezessete	Sunday the 17th
maio	May
flores de maio	May flowers
janeiro	January
janeiro de dois mil e nove	January 2009
fevereiro	February

o dia a mais do ano bissexto é dia vinte e nove de fevereiro

leap year day is February 29th.

março	March

março marca o início da primavera no hemisfério norte e do outono no hemisfério sul   March marks the start of Spring in the northen hemisphere and fall in the southern hemisphere

abril	April

agora é abril então mês que vem será maio   it is now April so next month will be May

junho	June

nós vamos casar em junho   we are getting married in June

julho	July

julho foi nomeado por Júlio César, que nasceu em julho

July is named for Julius Caesar, who was born in July

agosto	August
A escola está fechada em agosto	The school is closed in August
setembro	September
primeiro de setembro	September 1st
outubro	October
O dia das bruxas cai dia trinta e um de outubro	Halloween falls on October 31st
novembro	November
Ação de Graças, quinta-feira, vinte e quatro de novembro	Thanksgiving, Thursday November 24th
dezembro	December

We will be returning to childlike learning in Chapter Thirteen—"Learning Like a Child," as this lies at the heart of learning without mentally cramming.

Children are new to the learning process. They constantly see and experience things for the first time. They pause to listen to noises, try things over again until they master it, observe language until they can speak it, and ask if they don't know what something means. As we grow, we identify other ways to efficiently gather information.

However, with this, we sometimes stop paying attention to the details in our everyday lives that can provide us with fresh insight and information. Consider these tips on how to rekindle this childlike process for obtaining knowledge.

Take Time to Observe

Start paying more attention to the things around you. Take time to appreciate the clouds in the sky. Pay attention to how your coworker's, partner's, child's day is going. Become aware of the people you are in line with at the checkout counter. Have a purpose in your observation, whether it's to better understand human nature, be more effective with your time, or gain an appreciation for others.

Go Exploring

Coming across things you have not seen or experienced before can help you appreciate things like a child would. Hike on a new trail, visit a place you've never been, or try a different route to work. Look at the things you see every day with a new eye. Consider how you would perceive them if it was the first time you'd ever noticed them.

Learn from Everyday Moments

Pause to think about the things you do every day. This can be a good practice if you feel you don't have much opportunity to learn new things or if you feel you are not progressing in your education. Assess what you have learned during your day. For instance, did a conversation not go as well as you planned? Evaluate what went well and what could have been different. Consider how you can avoid a similar situation in the future. Write down the knowledge you have gained in a journal and review it occasionally. See where you have made improvements and how you have grown from these experiences. Note: This also helps with motivation.

Model Other People's Good Qualities

Start paying attention to the good qualities in others. Make a list of these traits and determine how you can emulate them. Work on the qualities one by one until you master them.

Take Time to Read

If you are busy, which most people are, look for ways you can incorporate reading into your schedule. Note: Unless you do not mind having to use a dictionary every minute, read dual-language Portuguese books (the translation sits alongside the page you are reading). These are a brilliant learning tool and hugely enjoyable. You will extend your vocabulary marvelously without even noticing.

Listen to audio books in your car, read on the bus, take a couple minutes of your lunch break, or put a book next to your bed where you can read a couple pages before you go to sleep. Or, to start you off, go on YouTube and type in search "Portuguese short stories." You will be presented with a whole host of short stories in Portugal Portuguese and Brazilian Portuguese that will not only be read out loud to you but you will also be supplied the text, enabling you to improve your reading and also your pronunciation and listening skills..

Try different genres. Ask people what their favorite books are and read them—not only will you gain more knowledge from the books, but you will learn more about those around you by understanding the books they like. Study famous and influential people and events in history. Read both fiction and nonfiction. Do some research on the life of the author. Find out what world and local events were taking place at the time the book was written.

Talk to Others

Share with others the things you are discovering, whether it's something you read in the news or heard about in another conversation. By talking about what you are learning, you can better understand and retain the knowledge you gain. It can also help you discover fresh perspectives.

Be a Hands-on Person

Find a new creative outlet. Research how to prune rose bushes and practice on the ones in your yard. Follow instructions on how to cut tile and create a mosaic table. Take something apart to ascertain how it works. Enroll in a continuing education course on NorthOrion, such as photography, ceramics, yoga, or bowling.

However you decide to do it, incorporate learning into your everyday routine. Select those methods that come naturally to you. Be willing to look at gaining knowledge as a child does, unembarrassed and optimistically. You may find that you can gain the same enthusiasm.

Please understand that when I say you should "learn like a child," I am not telling you to suddenly revert to wearing diapers and gurgling. I am talking about using some of the intuitive language learning processes that we use as children.

Adults have some advantages, which we will examine, and children have different ones. We can learn to use both precisely because we are adults.

One thing that is for sure: we don't have the same amount of time as children, so we need to optimize the time we do have to make time for language learning. But we can also utilize the time we spend doing mundane tasks to our advantage—listening to Portuguese, for example.

The other thing you can't do is fully immerse yourself in the language (unless you are moving abroad, of course).

Your brain is nothing like a child's. The latter is a clean slate, and yours is like a graffiti-covered wall. So, when we want to learn a language, we have to clear our minds as much as possible. This is where mindfulness is so useful—more on that later.

Adults have a huge advantage insofar as first - and second - language acquisition are basically the same thing.

Adults are further advanced when it comes to cognitive development. What's more, they have already acquired their first language. It gives them the advantage of having pre-existing knowledge!

All these factors influence the cognitive structures in the brain and make the process of second-language acquisition fundamentally different from the ones occurring when you learn a mother tongue.

As an adult, you have the huge advantage over a child of being able to learn the most important grammar rules of a language when you want instead of having to acquire them slowly and through trial and error.

As I mentioned previously, adults have pre-existing language knowledge. Children have to learn the mechanics of their mother tongue, while, as adults, we have a more developed grasp of how language works. After all, almost all of us know what conjugations or adjectives are. What's more, adults are outstanding pattern-finding machines—it's much easier for us to deduce and apply language rules!

To sum up—as adults, we can learn really fast. But it all depends on how much we want to learn. Motivation is key.

Learning requires effort. We know that instinctively, and it sometimes seems that there is no way around it. The trick is to make that effort enjoyable; then it will no longer seem like an effort. It is just like someone who is happy with their job compared to someone who hates it. One will wake up in the morning looking forward to going to work, and the day will fly by; the other will dread getting up and drag themselves to work, and the day will also drag on interminably. Your language learning experience is up to you, and as an adult, you have the ability to make it as enjoyable and as challenging as you wish. It is a mindset. Once you learn to **see** your mindset, you can start to **choose** your mindset. As with everything—you will reap what you sow.

CHAPTER SEVEN

PORTUGUESE GRAMMAR

Yes, I know, and I'm sorry, but you have to tackle it sometime if you want to master Portuguese. Remember, if you are not interested in learning grammar (I can't blame you, although it makes things a lot easier in the long run), you can simply skip this chapter. If you prefer, skip it for now and come back to it later or learn it in bits—doable chunks. I actually recommend skipping backwards and forwards as you will find it easier the more you learn the spoken language.

If grammar really does get you down and you find it a hard slog, see the next chapter, which is on motivation.

Portuguese grammar covers a lot of territory. To start writing grammatically correct sentences in the present tense, you need to know about masculine and feminine nouns, adjectives, and regular verbs in Portuguese.

Telling a Masculine Noun from a Feminine Noun in Portuguese
In Portuguese grammar, you need to be able to distinguish a noun's gender (either masculine or feminine) so that you can use the correct gender of any article or adjective

that describes it. You can follow some simple guidelines to help you identify a Portuguese noun's gender.

Masculine nouns usually end in an -o, and feminine nouns usually end in an -a. If a noun ends in a different letter, you can look up the word's gender in a Portuguese-English dictionary. At first, imagining that a door, a key, a chair and other "things" can be masculine or feminine can be very weird.

Making Portuguese Adjectives Agree with the Nouns They Modify

In Portuguese grammar, adjectives have to agree with the nouns they modify in both gender and number, no matter what.

Keep the gender of the thing you're talking about in mind: In Portuguese, every time you describe the noun with an adjective — like bonita (boo-nee-tah; pretty), simpático (seem-pah-chee-koo; nice), or grande (gdahn-jee; big) — you change the end of the adjective to make it either masculine or feminine. The adjective's gender should match the gender of the noun. Like nouns, masculine adjectives normally end in -o, and feminine adjectives end in -a.

In Portuguese, the adjective normally comes after the noun. This word order is the opposite of what it is in English, in which people first say the adjective and then the noun (red dress; beautiful sunset). It's one of the few differences in word order between Portuguese and English.

Here's how the nouns and adjectives get paired off. In the first couple examples, notice how the ending of lindo (leen-doo; good-looking) changes, depending on the gender of the noun it follows:

- homem lindo (oh-mang leen-doo; good-looking/handsome man)
- mulher linda (mool-yeh leen-dah; good-looking/beautiful woman)
- quarto limpo (kwah-too leem-poo; clean room)
- casa suja (kah-zah soo-zhah; dirty house)
- comida gostosa (koh-mee-dah goh-stoh-zah; delicious food)

Some adjectives are neutral and stay the same for both masculine and feminine nouns. These adjectives often end in -e rather than -o or -a. Adjectives in this group include inteligente (een-teh-lee-zhang-chee; intelligent) and grande (gdahn-jee; big).

Notice how the word inteligente stays the same, whether the noun is male or female:

- Ela é muito inteligente. (eh-lah eh moh-ee-toh een-teh-lee-zhang-chee; She is very intelligent.)
- Ele é muito inteligente. (eh-lee eh moh-ee-toh een-teh-lee-zhang-chee; He is very intelligent.)

If the noun is plural, just add an s to the end of the adjective: cachorros pequenos (kah-shoh-hooz peh-keh-nooz; small dogs).

Articles

Gender also applies to articles like: the, a, an.

- o (pronounced: ooh) means "the" for masculine nouns.

- a (pronounced: ah) means "the" for feminine nouns.

- o homem lindo (ooh oh-mang leen-doo; the handsome man)
- a mlher ulinda (ah mool-yeh leen-dah; the beautiful woman)
- o quarto limpo (ooh kwah-too leem-poo; the clean room)
- a casa suja (ah kah-zah soo-zhah; the dirty house)

Brazilians use the word the in front of nouns much more often than people do in English. When you'd say Books are fun, they'd say Os livros são divertidos (oohz leev-dooz sah-ooh jee-veh-chee-dooz; Literally: The books are fun). Brazil is big would be O Brasil é grande (ooh bdah-zee-ooh eh gdahn-jee; Literally: The Brazil is big).

Brazilians always use o or a before a person's name: A Mónica (ah moh-nee-kah), a Cláudia (ah klah-ooh-jee-ah), o Nicolas (ooh nee-koh-lahs), o Roberto (ooh hoh-beh-too). It's like saying the Steve, the Diane.

If a noun is plural, use os (ooz) if the noun's masculine and as (ahz) if it's feminine:

- os barcos grandes (ooz bah-kooz gdahn-jeez; the big boats)
- as flores amarelas (ahz floh-deez ah-mah-deh-lahz; the yellow flowers)

To say a, as in a hat or a table, say um (oong) for masculine nouns and uma (ooh-mah) for feminine nouns:

- um banheiro (oong bahn-yay-doh; a bathroom)
- uma pessoa (ooh-mah peh-soh-ah; a person)
- um livro (oong leev-doh; a book)
- uma mesa (ooh-mah meh-zah; a table)

To say some, use uns (oonz) if the noun's masculine or umas (ooh-mahz) if it's feminine:

- uns sapatos (oonz sah-pah-tooz; some shoes)
- umas garotas (ooh-mahz gah-doh-tahz; some girls)
- umas praias (ooh-mahz pdah-ee-ahz; some beaches)

When you make the plural of a word ending in m, such as um, the m always changes to an n: Um homem (oong oh-mang; a man) becomes uns homens (oonz oh-mangz).

Pronouns - an introduction

You use pronouns to refer to people when you don't say their names. Here's the way Brazilians do it:

- eu (eh-ooh; I)
- você (voh-seh; you)

- ele (eh-lee; he/him)
- ela (eh-lah; she/her)
- nós (nohz; we/us)
- eles (eh-leez; they/them — all males or males and females)

Brazilians don't have an equivalent of the English word it. Because "things" are either masculine or feminine in Portuguese, Brazilians refer to the thing or things as ele/ela/eles/elas when the thing isn't named. You don't hear this too often, because more often than not, Brazilians use the name of what they're talking about. But a mala (ah mah-lah; the suitcase) can become ela (Literally: she) if both speakers understand the context. Eu perdi ela (eh-ooh peh-jee eh-ah; I lost it) can mean I lost the suitcase.

If you're talking to a person who's a lot older than you (especially the elderly) or to an important person like a boss or a politician, instead of using você, use o senhor (ooh seen-yoh; Literally: the gentleman) or a senhora (ah seen-yoh-dah; Literally: the lady) to show respect.

Here are some sentences using pronouns:

- Eu falo português. (eh-ooh fah-loh poh-too-gez; I speak Portuguese.)
- Você escreve. (voh-seh ehs-kdeh-vee; You write.)
- A senhora é brasileira? (ah seen-yoh-dah eh bdah-zee-lay-dah; Are you Brazilian? — to an older woman)

CHAPTER EIGHT

MOTIVATION *(yawn)*

I don't know about you, but I usually need some pretty strong motivation just to get out of bed in the morning. Maybe, its age ... But I'm wandering off topic (onset of senility, no doubt). With me, it's usually the slow dawning of hunger and the yearning for caffeine, usually in tea form. If I can be bothered, I make it with (proper) loose tea in a teapot and pour it in to a bone china cup with a saucer. Why do I sometimes make it with a teabag in a mug and sometimes in a teapot and served in a china cup and saucer (a Royal Albert tea service if you must know).? Well, for one thing, it tastes a lot better when I make it with "proper" brewed tea and serve it in chinaware, but that really isn't the answer, as just dropping a teabag in a mug still produces a good cup of tea and saves a hell of a lot of time and messing about. The answer is really that when I can be bothered to make *real* tea it is usually tied in with that thing called "motivation".

I do have specific reasons for choosing to make real tea most mornings, which I will not bore you with. Some are practical and others are sentimental. The mornings when I don't make real tea also have their own fewer specific reasons, usually involving lack of time, or simply that I can't be bothered.

Sit back for a moment with pen and paper and list the reasons you would like to be able to speak Portuguese. Some reasons will spring readily to mind and will go at the top of your list, but others you might have to search a little deeper for and these are equally important. Have the list at hand, on a bedside table, perhaps, and give it a glance before going to sleep and upon awakening. The list may change after a while, but the reasons will be equally as important. They are your motivation, and you should reinforce them every day.

You don't have to use the same list all the time and writing it is just as important as reading it. Here is one that helps you to be positive about what you are doing. It is quite long as I have illustrated each point with an explanation, which you won't have to do as you will know what you mean. Feel free to take what you want from the list for your own use but don't forget to add your own. Only you know what really motivates you. I am indebted to Henrik Edberg from The Positivity Blog for the following list.

Get started and let the motivation catch up.
If you want to work in a consistent way every day, then sometimes you have to get going despite not feeling motivated. The funny thing I've discovered is that after I've worked for a while, things feel easier and easier, and the motivation catches up with me.

Start small if big leads to procrastination.

If a project or task feels too big and daunting, don't let that lead you into procrastination. Instead, break it down into small steps and then take just one of them to start moving forward.

Start tiny if a small step doesn't work.

If breaking it down and taking a small step still leads you to procrastinate, then go even smaller. Take just a tiny one-to-two minute step forward.

Reduce the daily distractions.

Shut the door to your office or where you are learning. Put your smart-phone on silent mode. If you are a serial web surfer use an extension for your browser like StayFocusd to keep yourself on track.

Get accountability from people in your life.

Tell your friends and family what you are doing. Ask one or more to regularly check up on you and your progress. By doing this, you'll be a lot less likely to weasel out of things or give up at the first obstacle.

Get motivation from people in your life.

Spend less time with negative people. Instead, spend more of the time you have now freed up with enthusiastic or motivated people and let their energy flow over to you.

Get motivation from people you don't know.

Don't limit yourself to just motivation you can get from the people closest to you. There is a ton of motivating books, podcasts, blogs, and success stories out there that you can tap into to up or renew your motivation.

Play music that gives you energy.

One of the simplest things to do when you are low in energy or motivation is to play music that is upbeat and/or inspires in some way. In the case of learning Portuguese, play some Portuguese or Brazilian music. There are also a lot of Portuguese-speaking radio stations online. For the moment, you can just run a search on Google and choose one that suits your tastes. Once your Portuguese has progressed you can become more eclectic with your choices.

Find the optimism.

A positive and constructive way of looking at things can energize and recharge your motivation. So, when you're in what looks like a negative situation, ask yourself questions like, "What's one thing that's good about this?" and, "What's one hidden opportunity here?"

Be kind to yourself when you stumble.

Don't fall into the trap of beating yourself when you stumble or fail. You'll just feel worse and less motivated. Instead, try this the next time: be kind to yourself, nudge yourself back on the path you were on, and take one small step forward.

Be constructive about the failures.

When you stumble ask yourself, "What's one thing I can learn from this setback?" Then keep that lesson in mind and take action on it to improve what you do.

Compare yourself to yourself.

See how far you've come instead of deflating yourself and your motivation by comparing yourself to others who are so far ahead of you.

Compete in a friendly way.

If you have a friend also learning Portuguese make it a friendly competition to learn some task first. The element of competition tends to liven things up. You could also add a small prize for extra motivation and to spice things up.

Remind yourself why.

When you're feeling unmotivated it's easy to lose sight of why you're doing something, so take two minutes and write down your top three reasons for wanting to learn Portuguese. Put that note where you'll see it every day.

Remember what you're moving away from.

Motivate yourself to get going by looking at the negative impact of not learning another language. Imagine where you will be in a year if you continue to learn. Imagine where you will be in five years if you continue to learn. Don't throw it away by giving up.

Be grateful for what you've got.

To put your focus on what you still have and who you are, ask yourself a question like, "What are three things I sometimes take for granted but can be grateful for in my life?" One possible answer could be: "I have a roof over my head, clean water to drink, and food to eat."

Mix things up.

A rut will kill motivation, so mix things up. Make a competition out of a task with yourself

Declutter your workspace.

Take a couple of minutes to clean your workspace up. I find that having an uncluttered and minimalistic workspace helps me to think more clearly, and I feel more focused and ready to tackle the next task.

Reduce your to-do list to just one item.

An over-stuffed to-do list can be a real motivation killer, so reduce it to the one that's most important to you right now (hopefully, learning Portuguese), or the one you've been procrastinating doing. If you like, have another list with tasks to do later on and tuck it away somewhere where you can't see it.

Don't forget about the breaks.

Try working for 45 minutes each hour and use the rest for a break where you eat a snack or get out for some fresh air. You'll get more done in a day and week and do work of higher quality because your energy, focus, and motivation will simply last longer.

Adjust your goal size.

If a big goal in your life feels overwhelming, set a smaller goal. And if a smaller goal doesn't seem inspiring, try to aim higher and make it a bigger goal and see how that affects your motivation.

Exercise.

Working out doesn't just affect your body. It releases inner tensions and stress and makes you more focused once again.

Take two minutes to look back at successes.

Close your eyes and let the memories of your biggest successes - no matter in what part of your life - wash over you. Let those most positive memories boost your motivation.

Celebrate successes (no matter the size).

If you're looking forward to a nice reward that you're giving yourself after you're done with a task, then your motivation tends to go up. So, dangle those carrots to keep your motivation up.

Do a bit of research before you get started.

Learning from people who have gone where you want to go and done what you want to do can help you to avoid pitfalls and give you a realistic time-table for success.

Take a two minute meditation break.

In the afternoons - or when needed - sit down with closed eyes and just focus 100% on your breathing for two minutes. This clears the mind and releases inner tensions.

Go out in nature.

Few things give as much energy and motivation to take on life as this does. Go out for a walk in the woods or by the sea. Just spend a moment with nature and, the fresh air and don't think about anything special.

What about learning a bit of Portuguese while just laying on the sofa?

Coffee Break Portuguese

This laid-back podcast does exactly what it says on the tin. The lively presenters give you ten-minute snippets designed to feel "like going for a coffee with your friend who happens to speak Portuguese". The podcasts go through the basics at beginner level right through to advanced conversations and are perfect for listening to while snuggled up on the sofa with a cup of something delicious. The basic podcast version is free for all levels.

https://coffeebreakacademy.com/p/one-minute-portuguese

CHAPTER NINE

BEST PORTUGUESE TV SHOWS

Have you ever thought about learning Portuguese by watching Portuguese-speaking TV shows?

Instead of sitting in a classroom memorizing irregular verbs, you could be learning Portuguese by sitting on the couch in your pajamas, munching popcorn.

But if it were really that easy, wouldn't everyone be speaking Portuguese by now?

And come to think of it, wouldn't you have already done it?

Watching Portuguese TV shows is a way of *adding* to your learning, but there are some pitfalls to watch out for. And you need strategies to make sure that you learn as much Portuguese as possible while you watch.

In this chapter, we will look at the best Portuguese TV shows on Netflix Amazon Prime, Apple, IMDb, RTV, SIC, TVI, Porto Canal, BandNews and TV Brasil, (if you do not have access to any of these platforms, you can use YouTube).

We will learn how to make the most out of these Portuguese TV shows. This includes:

- How to choose the right series so you'll get addicted to Portuguese/Brazilian TV—and to learning Portuguese!
- What to do when you don't understand (a common problem that's easy to solve when you know how).
- More than just chilling out: study activities to boost your learning with Portuguese TV shows.

By watching Portuguese TV shows, you'll constantly be improving your listening skills. And if you use the subtitles in Portuguese, you'll also improve your reading and pick up vocabulary more easily. It'll even improve your speaking as you'll get used to hearing common phrases over and over, and they'll come to you more easily when you need them in conversation

Best of all, you'll be learning and enjoying yourself at the same time!

At this point, you might be thinking, "Sounds great, but I've already tried listening to Portuguese/Brazilian TV shows, and I didn't understand anything."

And even if you do understand bits and pieces, watching TV in a foreign language can feel overwhelming. Where should you start? How do you know if you're learning?

By the end of this chapter, you'll have all the answers.

But first, let's look at the TV shows. First we will look at Brazil's offerings and then at Portugal's.

3%

Show Premise: Set in a dystopian future, 3% is a Brazilian thriller about young adults who get the opportunity to leave their deeply impoverished society and move to paradise. But only 3% succeed in making it there.

Learning Tips: This show was the one of the first original series in Portuguese, and is a great choice for language learners who want to hear how native speakers sound, while also enjoying a suspenseful and fun viewing experience. As mentioned above, switch the audio language to "Brazilian Portuguese [Original]" and watch with English subtitles (if you so choose).

The Mechanism (*O Mechanismo*)

Show Premise: This political drama features a police task force assembled to tackle corruption and money laundering in the Brazilian government. It's based on the real Operação Lava Jato ("Operation Car Wash"), an ongoing criminal investigation by the Federal Police of Brazil.

Learning Tips: Again, the default is the English dubbed version, which I strongly recommend avoiding. Change to the original Portuguese audio and enjoy this thrilling tale that can also teach you a few things about Brazilian politics and law enforcement.

Samantha!

Show premise: Samantha! is a Brazilian comedy about an '80s child star who tries desperately to regain her past stardom through a series of wild schemes.

Learning Tips: A silly and engaging comedy can be a great way to practice a new language because the emotions and facial expressions are often over-dramatized, making them easier to understand. Don't forget to switch the audio to Portuguese!

Super Drags

Show premise: An adult animated comedy, Super Drags is the story of three friends working in a department store by day and protecting the LGBT community as drag queen superheroes by night.

Learning Tips: While you may be tempted to watch the English dubbed version because it features the voices of some of the stars of RuPaul's Drag Race, resist the urge! For the sake of your language learning, watch the subtitled Portuguese version.

Most Beautiful Thing (Coisa Mais Linda)

Show premise: In this drama set in the 1950s, a young woman moves to Rio de Janeiro with her husband, only to realize he has abandoned her and taken all her money. She decides to stay in the city anyway and open a Bossa Nova club.

Learning Tips: Not only will this show help cement your language skills (once you switch that pesky audio to Portuguese, of course!), but it will also give you a sense of life in Rio in the 1950s.

Portugal Portuguese TV Shows

Mysteries of Lisbon

Show premise: Mysteries of Lisbon is a mini-series, which offers four 60-minute episodes – later turned into a two part movie – about the lives of a mother and son during the Liberal Revolution of 1820. This series won nine awards, including the Portuguese Golden Globe for Best Film, Best Actor and Best Actress in 2011 and the Satellite Award for Best Foreign Language Film in 2011. Mysteries of Lisbon shows a different side of Portugal – an older more mysterious side that is filled with secrets.

Learning Tips: Not only will this mini-series improve your Portuguese but it will give you a useful insight into Portugal's very interesting history. Once again, only watch the Portuguese version to improve your language skills unless you are a history buff.

Tales of Ladybug & Cat Noir

Show premise: If you aren't aware of Ladybug & Cat Noir as a series, really, where have you been hiding? The story follows two teenagers who by day attend the same school with one (Marinette) crushing painfully on the other (Adrien), yet by night fight crime side by side as Ladybug and Cat Noir. The twist if it isn't already obvious is that they have no clue about each other. There is a love story weaved through this that has captured the hearts of many an adult and teen!

Learning Tips: Animations always let us off the hook with languages. Change your audio preferences to Portuguese (European), and the subtitles too if you might need them, and you're all set.

Shadowhunters

Show premise: Shadowhunters takes place in The Shadow World, where the two 'sides' of the Shadowhunters and Downworlders are both united and torn apart by their similarities and differences. There is romance, action, and great commentary on our society told in a fantasy setting.

Learning Tips: You can watch in both European and Brazilian Portuguese since there is audio for both, though unfortunately there are no subtitles, so perhaps pre-intermediate learners and up would benefit most. Get watching; this show has won heaps of well-deserved praise for its representation and is a great choice for practicing your language skills.

Salvador Martihna - Tip of the tongue

Show premise: This is a standup comedy show with Salvador Martinha, an actor, writer, and comedian who apparently has his audiences doubled over in laughter. If you are more used to the standup comedy of the best comedians from the US and the UK, Salvador is just as engaging, and touches on just as many cringe worthy, hilarious, and controversial subjects.

Learning Tips: Our final choice of watches is one that is definitely for those more confident in their Portuguese. This is a great example of using media to pick up accents and colloquialisms though the pace is very fast. There are subtitles available in both English and European Portuguese to help you as you watch.

There are European Portuguese/Brazilian films and TV series being added to the aforementioned platforms all the time. Just check up on Google now and then to see what's streaming where and when.

How to learn Portuguese by watching TV shows

So now you've got some great Portuguese TV shows to choose from. You can watch them as a beginner, but since they're aimed at native speakers, you'll probably enjoy them more if you're already at an intermediate level or above as you'll be able to understand more of what's being said and pick up new words without too much effort.

That said, it is possible to enjoy Portuguese TV at lower levels, too; you just need a slightly different approach. In this section, you'll learn how to improve your Portuguese by watching Portuguese TV shows at any level.

You'll learn:

- How to choose the right series to get you hooked on Portuguese TV shows (and, consequently learn Portuguese!)
- Study strategies to make sure you're learning lots of Portuguese while you watch.

Which series should you choose?

The most important thing is to choose a show you really like. It's pointless choosing a drama/thriller like *The Walking Dead* if you don't like this genre. You'll get bored and drop it in no time.

Try to think about the kind of series you get hooked on in your native language and look for something similar.

How do you choose the right show for your level?

Probably, one of the first things you should do is take a little test to check on your present level and it's also a good thing to do on and off to see how much you are improving.

Go here to do your language test with the good people from The Listen & Learn Blog.

https://www.listenandlearnusa.com/portuguese-level-test

Some shows might not be the best option depending on your level. Let's take a popular show in English as an example: *Game of Thrones*. Being an epic story, it is a pretty complicated and demanding series, especially for beginners and "older" vocabulary is often used: words like "jester" and "mummer" which are practically useless at this stage. The fact that each episode lasts about an hour also makes it difficult to follow.

The best way to find out whether a Portuguese TV show is suitable is by putting yourself to the test. Choose a show and play an episode with both the audio and Portuguese subtitles on. Watch the episode for a few minutes.
If you can follow the Portuguese TV show, great!

From now on, you will only watch this and other series with the Portuguese subtitles on, listening and reading at the same time. This will help you memorize and see the usage of words you already know, and it will especially, help you understand what's being said by getting your ears used to these sounds while you read the words. If you find words or phrases you don't know, you can pause the episode and write them down or add them into a flashcard app like Anki (https://apps.ankiweb.net). Over time, this will become more and more natural, and when you feel comfortable enough, you may even abandon the Portuguese subtitles.

If you found it was too hard to follow even with the subtitles on, don't worry; you still have some options.
You might struggle to keep up, either because

- There are too many words you don't know.
- They speak too fast.

If you are not already aware of it, there's an amazing Chrome extension that will help. It's called Language Learning with Netflix and has interactive subtitles that you can click on to get the definition in your native language. It also pauses automatically after every line to help you keep up. Give it a try—it could transform your Portuguese!

Using a Portuguese TV show as a study resource

If you find Portuguese TV shows hard to follow even with the sub-titles on, then start with a learner series.
One of the reasons Portuguese TV series can be tricky to follow is that they're designed for native speakers—people who've spent their whole lives (at least 105,120 hours for an average 18-year-old) listening to Portuguese. No wonder they're tricky for learners!

But thankfully, there are some series that are aimed specifically at learners.

Practice Portuguese is a good place to start. You can find it on YouTube. Just type in "Practice Portuguese" in Google and follow the link to YouTube.

Another option is to try using subtitles in your native language, just to get your ears more used to the new sounds. One of the dangers with this technique is that you focus too much on reading the subtitles in your language and you don't benefit much from the Portuguese audio.

One thing you can do to get around this is to pay as much attention to the audio as you can. You'll notice that many words and expressions are repeated quite often by the actors.

When this happens and you don't know them, write them down in your study notebook or add them into a flashcards app like Anki (https://apps.ankiweb.net/). If you can't identify the words by ear, write down what's written in the English subtitles and use a dictionary to translate it or just Google it. Alternatively, you can flip to the Portuguese subtitles to see the expression written down.

In the meantime, keep studying Portuguese and learning more vocabulary, and over time, you'll notice that you understand more of the sentences without even reading the subtitles anymore. At this point, take the test above again to check if you can move onto the Portuguese subtitles phase.

Activities to boost your learning with Portuguese TV shows

Sometimes, when you're watching Portuguese TV shows, it feels magical. You're sitting there in your sweatpants, eating ice-cream and learning Portuguese at the same time. It's a win-win scenario.

But then a niggling doubt creeps in… Is this enough? Shouldn't I be doing more to learn Portuguese? While watching Portuguese TV can do a lot for your listening and speaking, there are more focused activities you can do to accelerate your learning.

The best bit—they still involve watching some TV!

The reality is that TV and films help you speak naturally and understand more.

If you spend all of your time just learning the slow and stilted dialogues that you find in textbooks, you'll probably end up speaking in a slow and stilted way.

Alternatively, if you listen to lots of realistic conversations in TV series and films, over time, you'll start speaking in a more natural way.

The same goes for understanding: if you only listen to learner materials, you'll get used to hearing a version of the language that's been watered down for gringos. You might get a shock when you hear people using it in real life!

On the flip side, if you get used to hearing realistic dialogues in TV series and films (even if it's tricky at first!), you'll be much better equipped to follow conversations in the real world.

I'm not suggesting you try to learn a language entirely by watching TV and films. Learner materials like textbooks and audio courses have their place in a language learner's toolkit. And as previously stated, speaking practice is essential to perfecting Portuguese.

Foreign-language TV series and films are like handy supplements that can help you bridge the gap between learner materials and how people actually talk.

What if I don't understand anything?

When people think of learning a language by watching TV, they sometimes imagine learning through something akin to osmosis—the idea that if you listen to a stream of undecipherable syllables for long enough, it will eventually start to make some sort of sense.

But it doesn't work like that.

To learn, you first have to understand the language. Once you get to a high(ish) level where you can pick out a fair amount of what the characters are saying, you can learn a lot from just sitting back and listening.

What if you're not there yet?

Before that, if you want to learn a language by watching TV and films, it's important to do activities that'll help you understand the dialogues. The following activities will help you do just that.

How to learn a language by watching TV and films: what you'll need

First, you'll need a film, TV series, or YouTube video with two sets of subtitles: one in the language you're learning and one in your native language. This used to be tricky, but with YouTube, Netflix, Amazon and Apple, it's getting easier and easier to find videos that are subtitled in multiple languages. Aim for videos where people speak in a modern and natural way (i.e., no period dramas).

One of the best of these is *Easy Languages* on YouTube. The presenters interview people on the street, so you get used to hearing natives speak in a natural and spontaneous way. What's more, the videos are subtitled both in the target language and in English.

Easy Portuguese (http://www.easyportuguese.com/) is particularly good as it has its own spin-off channel where they add fun and interesting videos a couple of times a week. If you're a beginner and you find these kinds of videos overwhelming (too many new words and grammar points), they also have a "super easy" series that you can use to get started.

Write what you hear

One super task to boost your listening skills is to use the videos as a dictation:

- Listen to very small pieces of the video (a few seconds each) and write down what you hear.
- Listen several times until you can't pick out any more.
- Compare what you wrote against the subtitles.
- Look up new words in a dictionary and write them down so you can review them later.

Often you'll see words and phrases that you understand on the page but couldn't pick out in the listening. You can now focus on the difference between how words are written and how people actually say them in real life.

This is your chance to become an expert at listening.

Make it your mission to become aware of these differences. Do speakers squash certain words together? Do they cut out some sounds or words completely? You may notice some things that native speakers have never realized about their own language and that teachers won't teach you.

Here is an example:
- In spoken English, "do you" often sounds like "dew," and want sounds like "one." So the phrase "do you want it" is pronounced like "dew one it."

No wonder listening is trickier than reading!

An awareness of these differences is your new secret weapon for understanding fast speech and developing a natural speaking style: the more you pay attention to these differences, the better you'll get at speaking and listening to the language as it's used in real life.

Translate it

Another invaluable task is to translate small passages into your native language and back into the language you're learning. After you've done this, you can check what you wrote in your target language against the original subtitles.

Ideally, you should translate the passage into your native language one day and back into your target language the day after so that you have to use your existing knowledge about grammar and vocabulary to recreate the dialogue (rather than just relying on memory).

This technique works because it gives you the chance to practice creating sentences in your target language and then compare them against the sentences of native speakers. In this way, you'll be able to see the gap between how you use the language and how the experts (the native speakers) do it. This will help you learn to express ideas and concepts like they do.

Comparing your performance to the experts' and taking steps to close the gap is a key element of deliberate practice, a powerful way to master new skills that is supported by decades of research.

Get into character.

One fun way to learn a language from TV and films is to learn a character's part from a short scene. Choose a character you like and pretend to be them. Learn their lines and mimic their pronunciation as closely as possible. You can even try to copy their body language. This is a great method for a couple of reasons:

- It's an entertaining way to memorize vocabulary and grammar structures.
- By pretending to be a native speaker, you start to feel like one – it's a fun way to immerse yourself in the culture.

If you are really up for it, record yourself and compare it to the original. Once you get over the cringe factor of seeing yourself on video or hearing your own voice, you'll be able to spot some differences between yourself and the original, which will give you valuable insight into the areas you need to improve. For example: does your "r" sound very different to theirs? Did you forget a word or grammar point?

Talk about it

A great way to improve your speaking skills is the key word method:
- As you watch a scene, write down key words or new vocabulary.
- Once you've finished watching, look at your list of words and use them as prompts to speak aloud for a few minutes about what you just saw.

As well as helping you practice your speaking skills, this method gives you the chance to use the new words you just learned, which will help you remember them more easily in the future.

Just relax and chill out

If you're feeling tired or overstretched and the previous four steps feel too much like hard work, you can use films and TV as a non-strenuous way to keep up your language learning routine. Get yourself a nice hot drink, make yourself comfortable on the sofa, put on a film or TV series and try to follow what's going on. Even if most of it washes over you, it's better than nothing.

While you obviously can't learn a language entirely by doing this, it's still handy because it helps you build the following four skills:

- Get used to trying to understand what's going on even if there's lots of ambiguity and you only understand the odd word (a useful skill to develop for real-life conversations!).
- Get your ears used to the intonation and sounds of the language.
- Become familiar with words and expressions that are repeated a lot.
- Stay in your language routine during times when you can't be bothered to study.

Don't underestimate the value of this last point: if you skip language learning completely during periods when you're tired or busy, you'll get out of the routine and probably end up feeling guilty. As time passes, it'll get harder and harder to get started again. But if you keep it up on those days, even by just watching a few minutes of something on the sofa, you'll stay in the routine and find it easy to put in more effort once you get your time and energy back.

CHAPTER TEN

NAVIGATING THE RESTAURANT

Who doesn't love to eat?

Explore delicious local foods while abroad—you won't be sorry! Or if you are lucky, go to a Portuguese or Brazilian restaurant in your home town.

Spending time at restaurants can really factor into your cultural immersion and Portuguese-language-learning experience.

Access to a fully equipped kitchen can be hard to come by while traveling, and you may well prefer to dedicate your time to seeing the sights rather than grocery shopping (though I'll be the first to tell you that exploring a local market can be extremely fun). Talk to locals, find out where the hot spots are, and ask about regional cuisine. People love to talk about food as much as they love to eat it!

No plans to travel? Join in on the fun by visiting a local Portuguese or Brazilian restaurant/bar with Portuguese-speaking staff who are usually more than willing to participate in your language-learning journey..

You may be worried about your pronunciation, especially if you are not familiar with phonetic spelling. Don't worry; there are a ton of resources online that can help you hear and speak Portuguese words. They are mentioned throughout the book and in the bibliography and at the end. Use them and practice out loud as much as possible.

Before you arrive at your destination, equip yourself with the following words and phrases so you can order your meal like a native Portuguese speaker!

First, the greeting according to the time of day:

bom dia - good morning

boa tarde - good afternoon

boa noite - good night/good evening

If you have a reservation:

Eu tenho uma reserva - I have a reservation

Include your name in the sentence:

Eu tenho uma reserva em nome de X - I have a reservation, under the name of X

When you don't have a reservation:

Ask for a table for two
Eu queria uma mesa para duas pessoas - I would like a table for two

Eu queria o menu, por favor - I would like the menu, please

Parts of the menu:

- entradas - appetizers
- sopas - soups
- pratos de carne - meat dishes
- pratos de peixe - fish dishes
- pratos do dia - today's specials
- sobremesas - desserts
- bebidas - drinks

O empregado de mesa (the waiter) approaches and you order:

Queria um Bacalhau à Brás - I would like a Bacalhau à Brás

Often the menu has the option of one portion and a half-portion you can also specify that in your order:

Queria uma dose de Bacalhau à Brás - I would like a portion of Bacalhau à Brás

A portion is usually very generous in quantity so a half-potion is plenty for a person who doesn't eat a lot or for children

The same structure works for ordering drinks. You will order a bottle of water:

Queria uma garrafa de água - I would like a bottle of water

If you don't specify anything else you will get a still mineral water. If you want sparkling water you must order it:

Queria uma garrafa de água com gás - I would like a glass of sparkling water

You can specify if you want something to eat or to drink:

Para comer queria... - To eat I would like...

Para beber queria... - To drink I would like...

So, to order something, you use the structure:

queria + the thing you want

Queria uma sobremesa - I would like a dessert

Queria um café - I would like a coffee

It's also important to mention that if you order a coffee, without any more information, you will get an espresso. Waiters sometimes assume you would like an espresso after you finish eating, especially if someone at your table has already ordered a coffee, so you might find yourself with an espresso in front of you, even if you didn't order it.

If something like this happens, or if you get a different dish from the one you ordered, you say. (we'll use coffee in this example):

Eu não pedi um café - I didn't order a coffee

Pedi is the past tense from the verb *pedir*, to order, in the first person singular.

Other things can go wrong like the food is too salty:

Está salgado - It's salty

Está muito salgado! - It's very salty!

What about if you have a question about a certain dish:

O que é Bacalhau à Brás? - What is Bacalhau à Brás?

Or if you don't understand what sides come with the dish:

Qual é o acompanhamento? - What is the side?

After your meal you wish to pay:

Queria pagar - I would like to pay

Getting the attention of the waiter. Raise your hand and say:

Desculpe! - Excuse me!
Olhe, desculpe, por favor! - Look, excuse me, please!

If you wish to pay by card:

Queria pagar com cartão de crédito - I would like to pay with credit card

Queria pagar com multibanco - I would like to pay with debit card

If you want to leave a tip. This is how to do it:

The waiter brings your change on a little plate. You decide how much of that you want to leave behind, or add something to it, if you feel that is not enough. Then, get up and leave!

If you paid by card and there is no change returning to your table, just leave your tip on the table, get up and leave!

If you don't leave anything at all that is also fine. Leave saying:

Muito obrigado - Thank you very much (if you are a man).

Muito obrigada - Thank you very much (if you are a woman).

Upon exiting:

Muito obrigado - Thank you very much (if you are a man).

Muito obrigada - Thank you very much (if you are a woman).

Bom dia/boa tarde/boa noite.

Need help remembering these words? You can use an online resource like **FluentU** (https://www.fluentu.com/portuguese/) to hear them given context and cement them in your memory.

FluentU offers a growing collection of authentic videos, including various clips, movies, music, and more. It's an entertaining way to immerse yourself in Portuguese the way native speakers really use it while actively building your vocabulary.

Understanding regional food traditions:

While traveling, always ask the locals

CHAPTER ELEVEN

PARTYING

You're in Brazil, and you just got invited to a killer party.

Portuguese, whether Brazilian or European, party expressions - like most slang - can be somewhat confusing if you've been learning a different dialect (or no dialect at all).

Learning slang invariably helps with learning Portuguese

No matter how advanced your Portuguese level is, if it's textbook-and-classroom Portuguese, it won't always help you on the streets. You need to learn some local expressions, some idioms, and definitely a lot of slang.

People who know plenty of slang sound like natives, understand what's going on around them, and feel less excluded when hanging out with the locals.

Learning a language through music, blogs, and novels is a great way to contextualize the local expressions, although they may not always tell you what those expressions mean.

How do people party in Portuguese-speaking countries?

Basically, like everywhere else in the world.

Considering how large the Portuguese-speaking world is and how many people live in it, we can't generalize on the party style. Some people party until morning, while others just share a few beers.

Either way, once people start drinking, the language loses all formality, and the slang comes out stronger than at any other time. In addition, it's quite common to hear Portuguese spoken very fast, which only becomes more obvious at parties.

For foreigners, this may lead to some uncomfortable situations. Trying to catch up with some high-speed conversations while juggling regional slang is a hard job to do.

If only you knew some basic party words and expressions… It goes without saying that these phrases are meant to be used by Portuguese learners who are old enough to responsibly enjoy adult beverages.

Where and when People Party

Everyone is familiar with Brazil's carnival, probably, the **biggest** party in the world! Mardi Gras is the only other people-party that comes close.

But there is another party that is celebrated throughout Brazil and is not as well-known outside Brazil. It is the Brazilian "June Party," in Portuguese "Festa Junina."
Through all the streets you can see the parties going on. Bonfires, music, food, dancing and traditional clothes everywhere.

"Quadrilha" is the traditional dance of the party. The typical "Quadrilha" dance started in the salons of the court of Paris (Quadrille) and came to Brazil after the colonization, where the Brazilians gave their own identity to the dance. The "Quadrilha" goes through several funny phases until the main couple, dressed as bride and groom, get married. The wedding is one of the most anticipated moments of the party and has priest, delegate and godparents present. The moment is full of humor and makes jokes with traditional weddings. The groom is practically forced to marry under pressure from the bride's father and despite some attempts, he can not escape marriage.
The clothes used in the dances are very traditional. Women wear flowered dresses with ruffles, boots, straw hats and braids in their hair. The men wear plaid shirts, jeans with sewn flaps, boots, and a straw hat. These are the most common clothes worn in Festas Juninas, inspired by the rural style of those who live in the countryside. However it varies a lot according to the region of Brazil.

Go wild on nights out in Lisbon

The epicenter of Portugal's entertainment industry is firmly fixed in Lisbon. Aside from the city's multitude of cafes and bars, the clubbing scene is legendary. Most restaurants, bars and clubs are located in the Bairro Alto, while trendier digs can be found in Santos and clubs for an older crowd are located in Alcântara and the docks. Part owned by actor John Malkovich, Lux (Armazém A, Cais da Pedra a Santa Apolónia) is probably Portugal's most fashionable nightclub.

Embrace nightlife on Portugal's Algarve

Some of the best nights out in Portugal are to be had on the sun-drenched Algarve. Here, bright young things spend their days sunbathing and swimming before decamping for an explosive night of partying along Albufeira's Avenida Dr. Francisco Sà Carneiro. The raucous fun of 'The Strip', as it's known locally, is just one side of Portugal's nightlife scene.

Join the spark in Porto

Porto is the second largest city in Portugal. It's a lively university town, so as you'd expect it hosts some of Portugal's best entertainment venues. The scene here is focused around Ribeira, Gaia, the university area, and Foz do Douro beach.

Some useful party vocabulary:

Come on, dude, let's party - Qual é cara, vamos festejar.

All right, now. Let's party! - Muito bem, vamos à festa.

Let's party, for real this time! - Vamos à festa, há tempo para a realidade!

Alright then, let's party - Tudo bem, então, vamos festejar.

Come on, Paige, let's party! - Vá lá, Paige, vamos festejar!
All right, Gadget, let's party! - Tudo certo, Gadget, vamos festejar!

We made it happen Now let's party all night! - Faremos acontecer, agora vamos festejar a noite inteira!

All right, everybody, there's only 13 hours left, so let's party! - Muito bem, pessoal, faltam apenas 13 horas, portanto vamos festejar!

Boate - nightclub/dance club (used in Rio de Janeiro)

Balada: - nightclub/dance club (used in São Paulo and to clubs that play techno)

Bar: - bar/pub

Boteco/botequim: - pub/neighborhood bar (usually with tables outside and food)

Baile funk: - Brazilian funk dance club/party

Entrada/preço: - cover

Gênero: - type of music

Comanda: - card or slip of paper used to keep track of your tab

Bebida: - drink

Chope: - beer from a tap

Cerveja: - beer

Lata: - can

Garrafa: - bottle

Caipirinha: - the national drink of Brazil, made with cachaça, sugar, and limes

Caipiroska: - a caipirinha made with vokda

CHAPTER TWELVE

TRAVEL

You've bought your ticket, your bags are packed, and you can't wait to begin your journey to a Portuguese-speaking country.

Now, there is a simple thing you can do that can have a very big impact on your trip.

Learn some Portuguese travel phrases!

Your trip will be so much more fun and meaningful if you can communicate with locals.

Below are the bare essentials, the most common survival Portuguese travel phrases and words you will need on your trip.

Useful Portuguese travel phrases every traveler should learn

Before you move beyond greetings, here is a tip for learning the words and phrases in this post: the best way to study them is to hear them in use.

Portuguese greetings

Portuguese-speaking countries are generally very polite, and you must always be courteous and say, "Hello" and "How are you?"

Do not worry about making mistakes; most people will try their utmost to understand you and to make sure you understand them. Just try your best, and they will be happy to reciprocate.

Greetings:

Olá / Oi (informal) — Hello

Como você está? / Como está? / Como tá? (informal) / *E aí?* (informal) — How are you?

Bem, e você? — I'm well, and you?

Foi um prazer. — It was good to meet you

Tchau / Até logo — Bye (literally "until later")

Obrigado/a — Thank you

Desculpa — Sorry or excuse me

Por favor — Please

Onde está o banheiro? — Where is the bathroom?

Com licença / Por favor — Excuse me (Note: You pronounce ç like a regular "s")

Preciso trocar dinheiro — I need to exchange money

Sim — Yes

Não — No

And, if you're really having trouble, you could always look for an English-speaker after all:

Fala inglês? — Do you speak English?

Getting around:

Que horas chega ___? — What time does the ___ arrive?

Sabe onde fica ___? — Do you know where the ___ is?

Carro — Car

Ônibus — Bus

Avião — Plane

Tren — Train

Taxi — Taxi

Bicicleta — Bike

Parada de ônibus — Bus stop

Pode me dizer como chegar no/na ___? — Could you tell me how to get to the ___?

Onde está o/a ___? — Where is the ___?

Hotel — Hotel

Quarto — Room

Museu — Museum

Parque — Park

Catedral — Cathedral

Cachoeira — Waterfall

Aeroporto — Airport

Esquerda — Left

Direita — Right

Reto — Straight ahead

Por aí — Around there

Em frente — In front of

Atrás — Behind

Rua — Road

Avenida — Avenue

Estrada — Highway

Faixa — Lane

Seguir — To follow

Virar — To turn (*Vira a...* — Turn… left/right/etc.)

Shopping:

Vou pagar só ___ dólares. Nada mais. — I will only pay ___ dollars. Nothing more

Quanto custa esta/o/as/os ___? — How much does this ___ cost?

Você tem ___? — Do you have ___? (Used when asking for things)

Camisa — Shirt

Saia — Skirt

Calças — Pants

Vestido — Dress

Sapatos — Shoes

Souvenir / Suvenir (less popular) / Lembrança — Souvenir

Portuguese Numbers:

Counting is good if you can spend a half-hour or hour learning some basic numbers. It really is just some simple memorization, and you can find numbers in any book on Portuguese or in your dictionary.

But if all else fails, pull out a pen and paper and write down the number you want and encourage the other person to do the same.

Miscellaneous Information:

Credit cards. Many places in smaller towns still do not take credit cards, so make sure you have enough cash with you.

You can ask if you can use a credit card:

Você aceita cartões de crédito?

If you have questions, you can always use a noun with a question. For example, you can pull out your credit card and say:

Cartão de crédito?

They will understand.

An all-purpose expression is:

Dobra não funciona!

It doesn't work! You can use this for a million circumstances. Just point at the shower or whatever and say, " *Dobra não funciona!"*

Practice saying everything aloud so that you will remember some of the phrases without looking and learn how to say these phrases relatively quickly and smoothly. Just hearing them spoken aloud will also help in your comprehension when people are speaking to you.

Take a small pocket dictionary with you. While you don't want to try to look up verb declensions in the middle of talking with someone, you can look up nouns quickly.

Better yet, take a phrasebook. There are tons of incredible phrasebooks (some that are partially travel guides), such as those offered by Lonely Planet, that are perfect for traveling and pulling out at a moment's notice. This way, if you ever forget one of your most important travel phrases, you'll be able to remind yourself.

And if you find a regional Portuguese phrasebook that focuses on your travel destination, you'll find even more useful phrases that locals love to use.

CHAPTER THIRTEEN

LEARNING LIKE A CHILD

As promised in Chapter Six, we are going to revisit what it means to *learn like a child* in greater depth.

Why is it that when we look back to our childhood, it seems that we effortlessly learned the things we truly wanted to?

There are a number of factors that we can look at individually.

- To start with, there seems to be a misinformed idea that as young adults, we have less on our minds and that this makes learning something like another language that much easier.

Mindfulness. Before you turn away in disgust and throw this book to the other side of the room shouting, "I knew it! He was a hippy all along. Now he is going to get me to cross my legs and hum OM," I am not going to ask you to do any of those things. If that is your thing, though, please feel free to do it, although I will remain dubious as to whether it will help you master another language.

I know mindfulness is a bit of a buzzword nowadays. A lot of people have heard about it but are confused about what it really means. This is not a book about mindfulness, so I am just going to go over the basics. It means focusing your awareness on the present moment and noticing your physical and emotional sensations without judgment as you are doing whatever you happen to be doing.

The benefits of mindfulness are plentiful. It increases concentration, improves self-acceptance and self-esteem, strengthens resilience, and decreases stress. In a world where we are continually subject to stress mindfulness can provide an oasis of calm.

Mindfulness (being mindful of what you do), can also help you to learn a language much more easily because a part of mindfulness involves unconscious concentration. To achieve unconscious concentration as an adult we have to practice it, unfortunately, as it is a skill many of us have lost. It is not as difficult as it sounds, and in fact, it is quite fun. Just take time out, if you get a chance, and watch some young children at play.

Look at how hard children concentrate in whatever game they are playing. They aren't making a conscious effort to concentrate; they are concentrating naturally, thoroughly immersed in the game. This is mindfulness in its most natural form, and this is what thousands of people pay hundreds of bucks every year to achieve once again.

Now, see what happens if you get one of the poor kids to stop playing and ask them to do a mundane and pre-set task like taking out the trash. Watch the child's attitude change: she's now, not just annoyed and resentful that she has been taken away from her game, but the concentration that was there when she was playing has gone. You could say her mind's not on the job, and you would be quite right. The mindfulness has gone, but it will return almost instantaneously when she resumes playing and having fun.

Games, puzzles, and challenges are all fun to us when we are young and we devote all our mind's energy to them wholeheartedly, and that is what we will try to recapture as we learn Portuguese.

When you are actively concentrating on learning Portuguese, it is a good idea to turn off all distractions except the method you are using to learn. By this, I mean all the gadgets we are surrounded by, such as: the telephone, radio, Facebook, Twitter, Instagram - you get the picture.

Multitasking is one of those words that is bandied about a lot nowadays - the ability to perform lots of tasks at the same time. But in this particular case, multitasking is a bad thing, a very bad thing. It has been proven that it isn't actually healthy for us and we are more efficient when we focus on just one thing at a time.

Take some deep breaths and focus all your attention on your breath. You will find your mind wandering and thoughts will distract you, but don't try to think them through or control them. Bring your attention back to your breath. It takes practice, and like learning Portuguese, if you do it every day, you will get better at it. Also, learning to breathe better will bring more oxygen to your brain.

Before you start any learning, take a few moments to breathe and relax. If you want, do some light stretching. This allows for better blood flow before studying. Better blood flow means more oxygen to the brain - need I say more?

When it comes to studying, do the same as you did with your thoughts: if you make a mistake, do not judge yourself Instead, acknowledge it and move on. Be kind to yourself at all times. You are doing an awesome thing - be proud of it. Remember that old saying: you learn through your mistakes. It is fine to make mistakes; just remember to learn from them and not get annoyed with yourself.

Just like with being mindful, be aware of the progress you are making with your language learning, but also be patient and do not judge yourself or compare yourself with others.

If you feel like it, smile a bit (I don't mean grin like a madman) as studies have shown that smiling brings authentic feelings of well-being and reduces stress levels.

You will find your mind wandering. Everybody's mind wanders. This is fine and completely normal. Just sit back and look at the thought. Follow it but do not take part. Be an observer, as it were. You can label it if that makes it easier to dismiss, for example, "worrying," "planning," "judging," etc. It is up to you to either act upon that and become distracted or let it go and focus on the task at hand - learning Portuguese.

CHAPTER FOURTEEN

SPEAKING PORTUGUESE

Learning Portuguese vs. Speaking Portuguese

Why do you want to learn Portuguese?

This question was put to the students using an app called Verbalicity (https://verbalicity.com). This is what they said:

"My wife is from Brazil, and I want to talk to her parents who don't speak a word of English."

"I'm going to Lisbon next April, and I'd like to be able to have some basic conversations with the locals."

"We get a lot of Portuguese-speaking patients at the clinic where I work, and I want to communicate with them better."

What do these people have in common? They all want to learn Portuguese so they can use it in the real world. In other words, they want to **speak Portuguese.**

Nobody ever wanted to learn Portuguese so they can stay in their house and watch *telenovelas* (Portuguese soap operas) all day.

So, if the goal is to speak Portuguese, then why do the majority of beginners start learning Portuguese using methods that don't actually force them to speak?

This is the single biggest mistake that most people make when learning Portuguese or any other language.

Most learning methods only teach you the "stuff" of Portuguese, like the grammar, vocabulary, listening, reading, etc. Very few of them actually teach you how to speak Portuguese.

Let's compare methods.

Methods that only teach you the "stuff" of Portuguese:

- Apps
- Audio courses
- Group classes
- Radio/podcasts
- Reading
- Software
- Textbooks
- TV/movies

Methods that teach you to speak Portuguese:

- Practicing with people you know
- Meetups
- Language exchanges
- Lessons with a Portuguese teacher online or in the real world

Many language experts, like Benny Lewis, have said that studying will never help you speak a language. The best way to learn Portuguese or any language involves more than just studying.

Let's say you are learning to drive for the first time. Your parents drop you off at the driving school for your theory class.

You spend many hours learning about traffic lights, left turns, parallel parking, and the dreaded roundabout. Your brain is filled with everything you'll ever need to know about driving a car.

Does this mean you can drive now?

No!

There's a reason why they don't give you your license right after you pass the theory test. It's because studying theory doesn't actually teach you how to drive.

You need to be behind the wheel, you need to get a "feel" for it with all of your senses, and you need to get used to making snap decisions.

Languages work in the same way.

To learn a language properly, you have to speak it.

Speaking: The one thing that makes everything else easier

You might be asking, "How am I supposed to speak if I don't learn vocabulary and grammar first?"

While it's true that a small foundation of vocabulary and grammar is necessary, the problem is that most beginners greatly overestimate how much they really need.

People spend thousands of dollars on courses and many months of self-study and still don't feel like they're "ready" to speak Portuguese. Speaking is something that they'll put off again and again.

Scientists from the NTL Institute discovered through their research that people remember:

90% of what they learn when they use it immediately.

50% of what they learn when engaged in a group discussion.

20% of what they learn from audio-visual sources.

10% of what they learn when they've learned from reading.

5% of what they learn from lectures.

This means that the best way to learn Portuguese is to start speaking from the beginning and try to use every new word and grammar concept in real conversations.

Speaking is the one skill that connects all the different elements of language learning. When you are speaking, you are actually improving every other aspect of the language simultaneously.

Speaking improves:

- Pronunciation
- Reading
- Writing
- Vocabulary
- Grammar
- Listening

Here's a breakdown of how speaking can improve your other language skills:

Vocabulary

Have you ever studied a word in Portuguese but then totally drawn a blank when you tried to use it in a conversation? Well, you will. Sorry.

This happens all the time because, although you can recognize the word when you see it or hear it, you can't naturally recall the word when you want to.

The only way for new words to truly become part of your vocabulary is to speak them repeatedly, putting them into real sentences that have real meaning. Eventually, the word will become a force of habit so that you can say it without even thinking.

Grammar

Let's say your friend asks you what you did yesterday, and you want to respond in Portuguese:

What is "To walk" in Portuguese?
"caminhar"

Ok, time to use past tense, but should I use preterit or imperfect?
Preterit because you're talking about a single point in time.

What is the conjugation for "caminar" for the first person?
"caminé"

Your answer: "Ontem eu andei na praia"

You may have studied all the grammar, but you would probably spend a good ten seconds thinking about this if you're not used to using grammar in conversations as this is different from the conjugated verb learnt from a book—things change when using phrases and you can only learn them by speaking.

Speaking is the only thing that trains your brain and speeds up this thought process until you can correctly respond in 1/10th of a second.

Listening

For many beginners, understanding native speakers is the number one challenge when learning Portuguese.

When you are having a conversation with someone, you are speaking and training your ears at the same time. You are listening "actively," which means you are listening with the intent to respond. This forces you into a higher state of concentration, as opposed to "passively" listening to Portuguese radio, for example, where you are simply taking in information.

Listening and speaking really go hand in hand.

Pronunciation

The first part of pronunciation is to understand how to correctly produce the sounds, which can be tricky, especially when it comes to rolling your R's properly.

Double r, r at the beginning of a word, r at the end of a word, and r before a consonant are all pronounced as h. Otherwise, r after a consonant but before a vowel or between two vowels is pronounced more like a single r in Portuguese.

Sounds complicated? It gets worse:
In cachorro, (for example) the rr is pronounced as an h. The word "preto" (black) is with the rolled r. Some words have it and some don't. You can only learn these particular words from listening and practice them by speaking.

Maybe at first, the words will make your tongue and lips feel strange, but over time, they will become part of your muscle memory until eventually it feels completely natural to say them.

Reading and writing

Portuguese is not a phonetic language, which means that the spoken words don't sound exactly as they are written.

Portuguese has 26 letters in its alphabet in total and those 26 letters are the same as in English. This is because Portuguese isn't a phonetic language. A phonetic language is one where you know how to say a word just by reading how its spelt. English, like Portuguese, isn't phonetic.

If you can say something in Portuguese, then you'll have no problem reading and writing it as well.

However, the opposite isn't true. If you focus on reading and writing, it will not enable you to speak better.

Why?

Because, when you're speaking, everything happens in **seconds**, whereas reading and writing happen in **minutes**. Only speaking will train your brain to think fast enough to keep up with conversations

80/20 your Portuguese

Also called Pareto's principle, the 80/20 rule states that 80% of your results come from just 20% of your efforts.

This principle is absolutely huge when it comes to the best way to learn Portuguese, and it has two major applications: **Vocabulary and grammar**

The Portuguese language is one of the most exotic languages in the world and its beauty lies in its words. The Portuguese language is estimated to be made out of a total of 250000 words with the largest Portuguese dictionary having over 171000 words.

Portuguese is the 5th most spoken language in the world and the 3rd in western world, surpassed by English and Spanish. Currently, approximately 250 million people speak Portuguese and Brazil corresponds to 80% of this total.

However:
- The 100 core Portuguese words make up nearly 65% of spoken dialogue

- The 1,000 most common words make up 88% of spoken dialogue

So, as you can see, you don't NEED to learn every single last word. Start by focusing on the most common words and the words that are personally going to be useful to you based on your interests and goals.

Just like vocabulary, you want to focus on the most common grammar rules and conjugations (ex. present, preterit, future, conditional, etc.). There are lots of advanced grammar rules that aren't used very often in everyday speech, so they are simply less of a priority.

Learning methods

It seems like there are a million ways to learn Portuguese these days, from traditional methods, like textbooks, to endless online resources. This creates a big problem for language learners: a lack of focus. A lot of people try to dabble in as many as five or six different learning methods and end up spreading themselves too thin.

Instead, **choose the one or two methods that are most effective (giving you 80% of the results)** and ignore the rest. Let's start by outlining some of the methods you could choose for your Portuguese learning.

Popular learning methods

Which methods work, and which ones should you not bother with? Here is a subjective low down.

The reasons why 99% of software and apps won't make you fluent

Take a second and think of all the people you know who learned Portuguese or any second language.

Did any of them become fluent by learning from an app?

Packed with fancy features, there are hundreds of apps and software out there that claim to be the ultimate, game-changing solution to help you learn a language.

- "Advanced speech recognition system!"
- "Adaptive learning algorithm..."
- "Designed by German scientists."
- "Teaches you a language in just three weeks!"

But do they really work? Is an app really the best way to learn Portuguese?

Or should you file this stuff under the same category as the "Lose 30 pounds in 30 days" diet?

The biggest software and app companies, like Rosetta Stone, Babbel, Busuu, and Duolingo, have all funded their own "independent" studies on the effectiveness of their software. In other words, they all paid the same researcher, who came to the conclusion that every single one of the apps was the best thing since sliced bread.

For example, the study for Babbel concluded:
"...Users need on average 21 hours of study in a two-month period to cover the requirements for one college semester of Portuguese."

This is no surprise because the fill-in-the-blanks, multiple-choice, one-word-at-a-time approach of software is the same kind of stuff you would find on a Portuguese midterm in college.

The problem is that just like software, college and high school Portuguese courses are notorious for teaching students a few basics while leaving them completely unable to actually speak.

At the end of the day, software and apps, just like the traditional courses you take in school, are missing a key ingredient: speaking with real people.

The best and fastest way to learn Portuguese is to spend as much time as possible having real conversations. It's the way that languages have been learned for thousands of years, and although technology can help make this more convenient, it cannot be replaced.

Software companies like Rosetta Stone have finally realized this, and in recent years, they've tried to incorporate some sort of speaking element into their product.

The verdict? Their top review on Amazon was one out of five stars.

Ouch! But if software and apps can't really teach you to speak a language, then why are they so popular?

Because they've turned language learning into a game. Every time you get an answer right, there's a little "beep" that tells you that you did a great job, and soon enough, you are showered with badges, achievements, and cute little cartoons that make it feel like you're really getting it. Of course, these things are also used to guilt you into continuing to use their app. If you stop using them, they start sending you pictures of sad cartoon characters telling you they will die because of your lack of commitment. Really? Do they think we've all turned into four-year-olds?

In the real world, playing this game shields you from the difficult parts of learning a language. You can hide in your room, stare at your phone, and avoid the nervousness that comes with speaking Portuguese in front of a native speaker or the awkward moment when you forget what to say.

But the reality is, every beginner who wants to learn Portuguese will have to face these challenges sooner or later.

The 1% of apps that are actually useful

Despite the drawbacks of software and apps, there is one type of app that can have a profound impact on your learning, and we have been here before:

Electronic flashcards (also known as SRS, or "spaced repetition systems").

I know I have already been over this, but they really do work. Ok, I know they don't sound very glamorous, and maybe the last time you saw a flashcard was in the hands of that nerdy kid in fifth grade that who nobody wanted to sit with at lunchtime.

But please, bear with me because this can totally change the way you learn Portuguese. Here's how a flashcard system works on an app.

Each flashcard will show you an English word, and you have to try and recall the Portuguese word. If you get it wrong, it will show you the card again in one minute, but if you get it right, it will be a longer interval, like 10 minutes or a few days.

A typical basic flashcard app is Anki. (https://apps.ankiweb.net).

Flashcard apps work by repeatedly forcing you to recall words that you struggle to remember, and as you get better, the word shows up less and less frequently. As soon as you feel like you're going to forget a new word, the flashcard will pop up and refresh it.

This system helps you form very strong memories and will allow you to manage a database of all the words you've learned, even those you picked up months or years ago.

You can also use flashcards for grammar concepts. For example, if you're having trouble remembering the conjugations for *"trazer"* (to bring), just make each conjugation a separate flashcard, like this:

- I bring > *eu trago*
- You bring > *tu trazes*
- He/she brings > *ele/ela/você traz*
- We bring > *nós trazemos*
- They bring > *eles/elas/vocês trazem*

By putting all your conjugations in all the different tenses into flashcards, you now have a way to repeatedly drill them into your memory.

The major advantage of flashcards is that all you really need is 10-20 minutes a day. Every single day, we spend a lot of time waiting around, whether it's for public transportation, in line at the supermarket, or for a doctor's appointment. This is all wasted time that you can use to improve your vocabulary. It only takes a few seconds to turn on the flashcard app and review a few words.

If you want to try this out, these are probably the two best apps out there:

Anki (https://apps.ankiweb.net)
The original, "pure" flashcard app.

Pros:

- Reviewing cards is extremely simple and straightforward.

- Very easy to write your own cards; it can be done on the fly.
- Plenty of customization options and user-written decks to download (although not as many as Memrise).

Cons:
- It can be a bit confusing to set up; you need to be tech-savvy.
- It doesn't provide reminders/motivation to practice daily.

Cost:
- Free for Android, computer.
- US$24.99 for iOS.

Memrise (https://www.memrise.com)

Flashcard-based app with modern features.

Pros:
- More variety for reviewing cards (fill-in-the-blanks, audio recordings, etc.).
- Offers a little bit of gamification (rewards, reminders) to keep you motivated.
- It has a big library of card decks written by other people and a large community of users.

Cons:
- Writing your own cards (called "Create a Course") is not as easy as Anki and can't be done on mobile.

- The review system works differently from traditional cards.

Cost:
- Free for all platforms (iOS, Android, computer).

Both apps come with standard Portuguese vocabulary decks as well as those written by other users. However, the real beauty of flashcards is being able to write the decks yourself. There is a big advantage to doing this, which you can see from the following steps:

When using pre-written flashcards

- You see a new word for the first time in your app and then review the word until you remember it.

When making flashcards yourself

- You get exposed to a new world through conversation, your teacher, or something you've seen or heard. You associate the word with a real-life situation.
- You write it into a flashcard, and by doing this, you're already strengthening your memory of that word.
- You review the word until you remember it.

As you can see, while making the cards yourself takes a bit of extra work, you get to control the words you learn and can focus on the ones that are more meaningful to you. Plus, the process of writing the word down acts as an extra round of review.

While it is true that flashcard apps have a bit of a learning curve, they are very easy once you get the hang of them, and you'll notice a huge difference in memorizing vocabulary and grammar.

Can you learn Portuguese by just watching TV and listening to the radio?

Countless beginners have tried and failed to learn Portuguese by what is known as "passive listening." Examples of passive listening include:

- Audio courses
- Radio and podcasts
- Movies and TV shows

The idea of passive listening sounds good on paper. You can learn Portuguese by listening to an audio course in your car on the way to work. Put on some Portuguese radio while you're making dinner and then sit down for an episode of *Killer Ratings* while you fold your laundry.

Except this doesn't work. Why?

Because learning a language is an ACTIVE process. You can't spend hundreds of hours listening to stuff in the background and expect your brain to figure it all out.

Now, many people will have a couple of objections to this:

I thought passive listening is how babies learn languages?

Let's assume out of simplicity that a baby is awake for an average of eight hours a day for the first year of its life. Through all the feedings and diaper changes, it is constantly being exposed to language because its parents are talking to it (and each other). So, by the time a baby says their first words at around the one-year mark, it has already had about three thousand hours of passive-listening exposure (8 hours x 365 days).

Now, how do you compete with that as a busy adult? Even if you squeeze in an hour a day of Portuguese radio into your daily life, it would still take you eight years to get the equivalent amount of language exposure. Who has the patience to spend eight years learning Portuguese?

Don't sell yourself short. With the right method and motivation, you can learn the Portuguese you need in months, not years.

If you incorporate a bit of Portuguese into every aspect of your life, then that's immersion, right? Isn't immersion the best way to learn Portuguese?

There are many expats who have lived in Portugal or Brazil for 5-10 years, and guess what? They STILL can't speak Portuguese.

These people have the perfect environment to learn, they can hear Portuguese everywhere when walking down the street, and every friend or acquaintance is someone they can practice with. But somehow, none of this seems to help.

Why?

Because they don't make an effort to speak.

Immersion is extremely effective, but only if you take advantage of the environment you're in and speak Portuguese every chance you get. Simply being there and listening is not enough.

As an adult, we have to learn languages actively. Most of us want to go from beginner to fluent in as short a time as possible, and passive listening is simply too slow.

If you're already listening to a lot of Portuguese, it doesn't mean you should stop. Try to do it actively, which means giving it 100% of your attention rather than having it in the background as you're doing something else.

Listening to radio, TV, and movies can be useful at a later stage. Increasing the amount of Portuguese you hear will speed up your progress when you are already at a conversational level.

But when it comes to learning Portuguese as a complete beginner, there are far more efficient methods.

How to practice Portuguese

We've already established that the best way to learn Portuguese for beginners involves speaking as much as possible. Let's go over the four main ways that you practice speaking Portuguese:

Speak with people you know

Maybe you have friends who are native Portuguese speakers, or maybe you are dating or married to one! If that person is the reason you wanted to learn Portuguese in the first place, it may seem like a good idea to practice with them from the beginning.

Pros:

- It's free.
- Practicing with people you know can be less intimidating than with a stranger, and as a result, you might be more willing to open up and speak (although, for some people, it has the opposite effect).
- They know you, and they like you, so they will probably be very supportive and patient with you.

Cons:

- You may not know anyone in your immediate circle of friends and family who speak Portuguese.
- When you make a mistake, they probably won't be able to explain what you did wrong. Most native speakers don't know the rules of their own language. Things "just sound right" to them.

- People have deeply ingrained habits. Once a relationship is established, it is really hard to change the language of communication. You can try to practice Portuguese with your wife, who is a native speaker, but more often than not, you'll find yourselves defaulting back to English because "it's just easier."
- Trying to practice Portuguese with friends and family can be frustrating. You're going to stutter, you won't be able to express yourself the way you usually do, and your wonderful sense of humor will suddenly become nonexistent. You'll feel guilty that you're being an inconvenience to them (although most of the time it's a bigger deal for you than it is for them).

Go to Meetups

Portuguese learners often get together a few times a week at a public place (usually a café) and practice speaking for an hour or two. A good place to find them is Meetup.com (https://www.meetup.com). Just do a search for "Portuguese + *the city you live in.*"

Pros:

- It's free.
- You get to meet new people in your area who are learning Portuguese just like you. Since you're all in the same boat, you can encourage each other and help each other stay accountable.

- You can share learning tips with each other, like what's working and what's not.
- If you need an explanation for a grammar concept, chances are someone in the group knows and can explain it to you.

Cons:

- You'll only be able to find meetups in big cities. If you live in a smaller city or town, then you're out of luck.
- It's not great for shy people. Speaking in a group of 10-15 people can be pretty intimidating.
- What often happens at meetups is that you all sit around a table and two or three people will end up doing most of the talking (remember the 80/20 rule?) while the rest just sit there and listen.
- Everyone is at different levels of fluency, so you could find yourself talking to someone who is way more advanced than you are, and you may end up boring them. Unfortunately, some groups don't let complete beginners join for this very reason.
- If you are just starting out and don't feel confident in speaking, you might end up doing a whole lot listening and not much talking. You get much better value out of meetups if you are already somewhat conversational.

Language exchanges
The basic idea is to find a native Portuguese speaker who is trying to learn English. You meet in person or have a Skype

call (or something similar) where you split your time practicing both Portuguese and English. The easiest way to find a partner is through online exchanges like My Language Exchange (https://www.mylanguageexchange.com) and Conversation Exchange (https://www.conversationexchange.com).

Pros:

- It's free.
- You can get exposure to a lot of different people who come from different Portuguese-speaking countries and with different backgrounds.

Cons:

- It can be very time consuming to find the right language partner. It can take a lot of trial and error.
- You only get to spend 50% of your time speaking in Portuguese.
- Your partner won't be able to speak English well, so it can be tough to communicate if both of you are beginners.
- Your partner probably won't be able to explain Portuguese grammar to you, and you won't be able to explain English very well, either. For example, can you explain when you should use "which" vs. "that"? Or how about "who" vs. "whom"?
- Partners can be flaky since there is no paid commitment, and some people simply don't show up

at the agreed time (happens more often in online exchanges).

Professional Portuguese teachers

These days it is far more convenient to find a Portuguese teacher online, and believe it or not, this can be even more interactive than being face-to-face. You participate in your lessons via Skype from the comfort of home and on your own schedule. This is how many people prefer to learn Portuguese.

Pros:

- A good teacher is like having your own coach or personal trainer. They want you to succeed, and they are there to support you and offer motivation and advice. It is much easier to learn Portuguese when someone is there to hold you accountable.
- A teacher is a trained professional. They have comprehensive knowledge of both Portuguese and English grammar, so they can explain to you the difference between the two, and provide a lot of useful examples to help you understand difficult concepts.
- Teachers know how to correct you when you make a mistake, but not so often as to interrupt the flow of conversation. Talking to a teacher just feels natural.
- Even if you're the shyest person in the world, a good teacher knows how to coax you into speaking and how to build your confidence. You don't have to

- worry about making mistakes, you'll no longer feel embarrassed, and ultimately, you'll have fun.
- A teacher can quickly figure out your strengths and weaknesses and come up with a learning plan to address them.
- They will design a customized curriculum for you based on your learning goals and interests. This ensures that whatever they teach will be very meaningful to you.
- A good Portuguese teacher should provide you with all the materials that you'll need, so you won't have to buy a textbook or spend time looking for grammar exercises.
- While a good chunk of your time is spent having conversations, your teacher will introduce exercises that cover all language skills, including pronunciation, reading, writing, and listening.

Cons:

- Just like language exchange partners, it can take some trial and error to find the right teacher. This is true especially if you are looking through an online teacher directory that doesn't do a great job of screening their teachers. You can waste hours scrolling through teacher profiles (which all seem to have five star ratings), only to be disappointed with the one you chose.
- Teachers aren't free. But getting a private teacher is a lot more affordable than you think...

Sure, there are plenty of "high end" teachers who will try to charge you as much as US$60-80/hour. On the "low end," you can probably find someone for less than US$10/hour, although they are usually unqualified tutors who can barely explain things better than your average native speaker.

Verbalicity has a good offer of "high-end" teaching for as little as US$15/hour. You can try out the first lesson for free. Go to: https://verbalicity.com

Of course, there are plenty of people who have learned Portuguese without a teacher. Doing a language exchange or going to a meetup is certainly better than not speaking at all, but it will take much longer to learn, and you may be tempted to give up in the process.

So, if you've got a busy schedule and want to learn Portuguese fast, then getting a teacher is definitely the best way to go.

Road Map: Zero to Conversational

We've just isolated some of the key concepts and methods that make up the best ways to learn Portuguese. Now let's go through the three stages of learning. For each stage, we'll recap what the main goals and recommended method of learning are and offer some more tips on how to progress as quickly as possible.

Stage 1: Introduction

This stage is for absolute beginners. If you already have some knowledge of Portuguese or are used to hearing it, then you can skip to the next stage.

Objective:

The idea is to get a brief introduction to Portuguese with the goal of familiarizing yourself with the following:

- What spoken Portuguese sounds like.
- How it feels to pronounce Portuguese words.
- A few basic phrases.

This helps you acclimatize to learning a new language and gets you used to listening and speaking right away.

After this stage, you probably will have some basic phrases under your belt, like "My name is...", "Where are you from?" and "What time is it?"

How to do it:

Start with a free audio course or one of the popular apps. Ideally, it should be a guided course that's easy to follow. Here are some examples:

- One Minute Portuguese audio course, Portuguese Survival Course
- Get Memrise (https://www.memrise.com) and start using their basic Portuguese course, or use other free apps like Duolingo (https://www.duolingo.com).

"Wait," you are no doubt be saying to yourself, "didn't he say that apps can't teach you a language?"

That's true. But I didn't say they couldn't help, and at this point in time, all you're trying to do is get your bearings and get comfortable with listening and repeating.

You probably only need about 30 minutes a day, and this introductory stage should last no more than a few weeks.

Afterward, you can cut down or stop using these resources altogether because, although they are fine as an introduction, they are slow and inefficient. You should move on to better options, which we'll cover next.

Tip for this stage:

Focus on pronunciation

Try to get your pronunciation right from the very beginning. When you hear the Portuguese recording, make sure you repeat it out loud.

At first, repeat each word slowly, syllable by syllable, until you can mimic the sounds almost perfectly. If necessary, record yourself speaking and listen back.

Once you're satisfied that you're saying it right, then repeat it over and over again until it feels natural.

Stage 2: Beginner

Objective:

At this stage, the goal is to build a solid foundation for yourself in terms of basic grammar and vocabulary, put your thoughts into complete sentences, and be confident enough to talk to people.

At the end of this stage, you want to be able to have basic conversations that involve exchanging information, asking for things, and talking about work, family, and your interests.

Effectively, you want to be at an upper-beginner level.

How to do it:
For the beginner stage, the best way to learn Portuguese is to choose one of these two options:

Option 1:

- Textbook
- Speaking practice: friends, meetups, exchanges, Skype.
- Flashcards (optional)

Using a textbook might seem old-fashioned, but it is still probably the best way for a beginner to learn the grammatical rules of Portuguese. The reason why a textbook is effective is that it teaches you in a structured way. It takes you through a progression that slowly builds on each concept, step by step.

For each chapter of the textbook that you go through, study the dialogues and make sure you do all the practice exercises. Ideally, you should try to find additional exercises online related to the concept you just learned.

Just like most forms of learning, a textbook can't actually teach you to speak. So, for each concept you learn, you need to be practicing it with real people.

You can use a combination of friends, meetups, or language exchanges to get your practice in. At this point, you are not having full conversations yet (nor should you try to). Try practicing phrases and some short dialogues or scenarios. But nevertheless, you should aim for one to two hours per week of speaking practice.

Option 2:

- Learn with a Portuguese teacher in person or online
- Flashcards (optional)

When you learn with a teacher, you get step-by-step guidance and speaking practice all in one package.

A good Portuguese teacher will send or give you textbook materials and all the practice exercises you'll ever need, so there is no need to look for materials on your own. You even get homework, just like in school.

A teacher can also explain grammar to you in different ways and answer your questions if you don't understand. This is a big advantage over someone who is just studying on their own.

Being able to practice what you learned immediately through speaking is another advantage. For example, you might spend the first half of a lesson going over the conjugations of the Imperfect tense and then spend the second half the lesson practicing it verbally through question and answer, storytelling, and other fun exercises.

Flashcards

It is never too early to start using flashcards to help you remember words.

But especially if you've chosen Option 1, it might be a little overwhelming to be studying while trying to find practice opportunities, and you don't want to add another method like flashcards to distract you from that.

Remember the 80/20 rule. It is better to focus on a few things that have the highest impact.

But if you feel like you're having trouble remembering new words or grammar conjugations, then it's probably time to incorporate flashcards into your routine.

Tips for this stage:

Don't jump ahead

It might be tempting to immediately work your way through a textbook from cover to cover, but this will just overload you with information.

A lot of people make the mistake of diving too deep into the grammar without making sure that they fully understand and have practiced each concept before moving on to the next. If in doubt, spend more time reviewing what you've already learned.

Be strategic about your vocabulary

Focus on memorizing the most useful words that will make it easier for you to practice speaking. Highly useful words include "power verbs" and "connectors."

An example of a power verb:

Ser   To be

Conjugation of the Verb Ser in the Present Tense:

Eu sou

Você é

Ele/Ela é

Nós somos

Vocês são

Eles/Elas são

When to Use the Verb Ser
- Use Ser for Introductions:

Eu **sou** Luciana. - I am Luciana

Meu nome **é** Luciana. - My name is Luciana.

Meu nome **é** Luciana. - My name is Luciana.

- Use Ser to express nationality or place of origen:

Eu **sou** brasileira. - I am Brazilian.

Dani **é** do Brasil. - Dani is from Brazil.

Eles **são** americanos. - They are Americans.

- Use Ser to state your profession

Eu **sou** professora. - I am a teacher.

Márcio **é** médico. - Márcio is a physician.

- Use Ser to indicate marital status

Joana **é** casada. - Joana is married.

Nós **somos** solteiros. - We are single.

Eles **são** divorciados. - They are divorced.

Examples of connector words:
Connecting (or transitional) phrases connect ideas within a sentence. They are especially useful in spoken Portuguese to fill the gaps between uttered ideas. Here are some very common ones:

- **Acho** – I think, I guess.

Acho que deixei as chaves do escritório em casa. – I think I left the office keys at home.

- **Apesar de** – in spite of the fact, although.

Apesar de não ter dinheiro nenhum, ele saiu de férias. – In spite of the fact that he didn't have any money, he went on vacation.

- **Assim** – in this manner, like this, like that

Você tem que fazer as coisas assim. – You must do things like this.

- **Como vou dizer** – how should I put it

Ele é meio – como vou dizer – preguiçoso. – He's kind of – how should I put it – lazy.

- **De qualquer jeito, de qualquer maneira** – in any case

Não sei se vou ou não. Mas eu te ligo, de qualquer maneira. – I don't know if I'll go or not. But I'll give you a call, in any case.

- **De jeito nenhum, de maneira nenhuma** – no way, under no circumstances

Você não vai fazer isso de jeito nenhum! – No way you're going to do this!

- **Digamos** – let's say

Vamos nos encontrar, digamos, às oito e meia. – We'll meet, let's say, at eight-thirty.

- **Embora** – even though

Embora fizesse frio, fui à praia. – Even though it was cold, I went to the beach.

If you master these types of words, your speech will come out more naturally, and it will make you sound more fluent than you actually are at this point. This can give you a much-needed boost of confidence because, at this stage, it can still be scary to be out there talking to people.

Intermediate

Objective:

This stage is all about expanding your horizons. It's about greatly increasing your vocabulary, comprehension skills, and confidence in using Portuguese in a variety of situations.

At the end of this stage, you want to be able to express yourself freely and talk about different topics, like what's happening in the news, your hopes and dreams, or your opinion on a particular subject.

You're still going to make plenty of mistakes, and your grammar won't be perfect, but the goal is to be able to get your ideas across, whatever they may be. If you can do that, you'll reach the upper intermediate level and be considered **conversationally fluent**.

Some may choose to improve their Portuguese even further, to more advanced levels, but for many people, this is the level where you can fully enjoy the rewards of being able to speak Portuguese.

How to do it:

Based on the two options from the beginner stage, we can make a few adjustments for the intermediate level:

Option 1:

- Speaking practice (*friends, meetups, exchanges*)
- Reading and listening
- Flashcards

- Textbooks (*optional*)

Option 2:

- Learn with a Portuguese teacher
- Reading and listening
- Flashcards

Speaking practice

To move into the intermediate stage, speaking becomes even more important. By now you should be ramping up your speaking practice to a **minimum of two to three hours per week**.

Whereas you were previously practicing short phrases or dialogues, you should now be able to have more full-fledged conversations because you know more vocabulary and grammar.

If you are learning with a teacher, you should know them pretty well by now, so you can have deeper conversations about more diverse topics. Your teacher can also start to speak a little bit faster to help train your ear.

Active Reading/Listening

This is the stage where active reading and listening start to shine. You know enough Portuguese now that you can really take advantage of movies, TV, radio, podcasts, books, and articles.

You won't understand 100% of what you read and hear. Heck, maybe you only understand 50-60% at this point, but that is enough to get the gist of what is going on. If you're watching TV shows or movies, turn on Portuguese subtitles (Netflix is great for this). Reading and listening at the same time will get you the best results.

Try to find material that is interesting to you. This way, you can enjoy the process of listening and reading, which can become a source of motivation. You'll also pick up Portuguese that is relevant and useful to you personally.

Remember, "Active" means giving it your full attention. Try your best to understand it and pay attention to the grammar and vocabulary and the context that they are being used. If there is anything you don't understand, write it down so you can look it up later, or ask your teacher during your next lesson.

Flashcards

A big part of going from beginner to intermediate is significantly increasing your vocabulary. By now, you will have already learned all the "easy" words, and to further build your vocabulary, you need to be very deliberate about remembering all the new words you are exposed to every day.

Using flashcard apps like Anki or Memrise can really help commit them to memory. You can practice in five-minute chunks (while waiting for the bus, etc.) for a total of 10-20 minutes a day to get great results.

Textbook

A textbook is not mandatory at this point. You've learned most of the important grammar, and now the focus should be to practice it until you can use it fluidly.

Of course, there are always more advanced grammar concepts to learn, but they tend to be used very sparingly in everyday conversations.

Tips for this stage:

Learning formula

Your "routine" for learning new material should look something like this:

- You're exposed to new Portuguese vocabulary and grammar through your teacher and textbook or by listening and reading.
- Review it using flashcards.
- Speak it until it becomes second nature.

For example, you hear the phrase "me deixa louco" (drives me crazy) on a Portuguese TV show.

You look up the meaning and then create a new flashcard in Anki.

The next day, the flashcard pops up, and you review it.

A few days later, you head to your Portuguese meetup, and during a conversation about music, you say, "Essa música me deixa louco!" (That song drives me crazy!)

Staying Motivated

When you reach the intermediate stage, you may feel like you're not progressing as fast as you did before. In fact, there will be times where you feel like you aren't improving at all.

This is the classic "dip" that comes with learning any skill, and Portuguese is no exception.

This happens because you've already learned a lot of the "low-hanging fruit." What you are learning now is more incremental and takes longer for everything to click in your mind.

To overcome the dip, you need to trust the process and be disciplined when it comes to the learning formula.

Your teacher can really help you stay motivated by creating a plan that guides you to new things you should learn and older concepts you should be reviewing, as well as giving you feedback on what you are doing well and what you need to improve on.

Time Frame

So, how long does it take to learn Portuguese using this road map?

I'm not going to lie to you and say that you can become fluent in 30 days. Maybe some people can, but most of us lead busy lives, with jobs, families, and other responsibilities competing for our time.

If you are learning with a Portuguese teacher (Option 2), I believe that you can go from zero to conversationally fluent in **8–12 months** using the methods in this road map.

This assumes that you can spend **one hour per day** working on your Portuguese, whether that's the actual Portuguese lessons themselves, reviewing flashcards, or actively listening and reading.

This timeframe is just an estimate because, obviously, everyone learns at a different pace. Of course, the more time you dedicate to learning Portuguese, the faster you'll progress.

If you decide to go at it alone (Option 1), it will take a lot longer. But if you follow the best way to learn Portuguese as outlined in the road map, stay disciplined, and make sure you consistently get enough conversation practice, you'll get there eventually.

Final Thoughts

Absolutely anyone can learn Portuguese.

It doesn't matter whether or not you have a talent for languages or whether you are a naturally fast learner.

At the end of the day, learning Portuguese is about motivation, focus, and time.

If you've got all three of these things and you commit to speaking rather than just learning the "stuff" of Portuguese, then you simply cannot fail.

And of course, don't forget to have FUN! The process should be as enjoyable as the end goal.

CHAPTER FIFTEEN

LEARNING WITHOUT TRYING

Remember the story about the lazy bricklayer way back in Chapter One? Well, to recap, the lazy way, or the way that involves the least amount of work, is most often the smartest way to do things.

Do the things that involve the least amount of work when learning a language. Engage in effortless language learning, not completely effortless, of course, but as effortless as possible.

The word "effortless" in this context is borrowed from two sources. One is AJ Hoge, who is a great teacher of English. His channel and website are both called Effortless English. The other source is Taoist philosophy.

Effortlessness and the Parable of the Crooked Tree

When the linguist Steve Kaufmann (who, incidentally, can speak over 20 languages) wrote his book *The Linguist: A Personal Guide to Language Learning*, he began with what he called "The Parable of the Crooked Tree."

The author of the parable was Zhuangzi, an early exponent of Taoism, a school of Chinese philosophy from over two thousand years ago. Zhuangzi's basic principle in life was to follow what was natural, what was effortless, and not try to force things.

Typically, the Taoist philosophy was in opposition to Confucianism, which prescribed rules of what you should and shouldn't do to be a great person. Confucianism is full of admonishments on how you should behave. As is often the case with prescriptive philosophies or religions, these "commandments" attempt to set the boundaries of correct behavior. Zhuangzi was different. He advised people to follow their own natures and to not resist the world around them. This effortless non-resistance would help them learn better and be happier.

In Zhuangzi's parable of the crooked tree, his friend Huizi tells him that a tree they are both observing is crooked because the lumber is not good for anything, like Zhuangzi's philosophy.

"Neither your philosophy nor the tree is good for anything," says Huizi.

Zhuangzi replies, "You say that because you don't know how to use them. You have to use things for the purpose intended and understand their true nature. You can sit underneath a crooked tree and enjoy its shade, for example. If you understand the true nature of things, you will be able to use them to achieve your goals."

In the lumber business, sometimes those gnarly old trees produce very expensive and decorative wood. Compared to trees in a planted forest, their wood is less uniform and less suitable for industrial end uses. We just have to accept these more individualistic trees as they are and appreciate what they bring. Zhuangzi defends his philosophy, saying it is useful if we accept its nature and know how to use it.

Zhuangi's philosophy was based on effortlessness, "wu wei" (无为) in Chinese. In other words, if you want to learn better, stop resisting; go with the flow. That has always been my approach. Language learning does require some effort, of course, but we learn best when effort is minimized and pleasure is maximized.

Let's look at something that requires effort but is also usually enjoyable: reading.

If you are reading in a language that you read well and you come across a few unknown words, you usually don't look up those unknown words in a dictionary because it's too much trouble and you have usually worked out the meaning because of the context.

So, what happens if you are reading something in Portuguese as a beginner and have to constantly resort to dictionaries? They are no longer the learning aid they once were but become a chore and a block to enjoying reading in the way you are accustomed. And what's worse, if you don't memorize these new words' meanings, you will keep on getting bogged down. So, is there a better or easier way to start off reading in Portuguese - an effortless way?

Thankfully, yes, there is. It is called LingQ (https://www.lingq.com/en). You can read in Portuguese using LingQ on your computer, laptop, iPad, or smartphone.

When you look up a word in LingQ, it's highlighted. The word then appears highlighted in any subsequent material so you are reminded that you've looked it up before. You can see the meaning straight away, and eventually it becomes part of you, without any effort.

You are not just looking words up in a dictionary and then forgetting them. You are creating your own personal database of words and phrases for easy review as you continue reading.

Steve Kaufmann highly recommends this as a way of learning a language, and he should know. He has similar practical thoughts on grammar:

When I read grammar – and I believe we should occasionally read grammar rules as it helps give us a sense of the language – I don't try to remember anything.
I don't try to learn or understand anything. I just treat it as a spark, an exposure of something that might help me eventually get a sense of the language. I don't worry about grammar. I know it will gradually become clearer for me.

Have you ever noticed how some people can learn languages effortlessly (Steve Kaufmann would be one), getting to fluency faster with pen and paper than others do with a bag full of textbooks and phone-full of learning apps?

Everything about their learning seems effortless, and every new word and expression they learn is used with utmost confidence.

What is it about these individuals that sets them apart?

Every language learner strives for this effortlessly cool way of learning, where study ceases to be a chore and language usage becomes commonplace.

While it may seem like these individuals were born with a natural linguistic talent, it actually, all comes down to a few simple habits these super-learners integrate into their daily life.

Here's a short list, along with some tips on implementing these habits in your daily life and becoming the confident speaker you want to be.

Note: You do not have to follow these recommendations exactly; adapt them to your lifestyle and unique personality.

Review before learning, even if it means you don't have time or energy to learn more.

Effective language learners know that what you don't review, you forget forever, and forgetting means that all that time you've spent learning the new word or expression has been put to waste.

That is why you should always prioritize reviewing above learning and start every study session by going over your past notes and flashcards.

That way, if you realize halfway through that you're just too exhausted to make the progress you hoped for, you've at least made sure you don't regress by activating all the connections already in your brain!

Tip: Never learn something new before you review what you know already.

Study a little bit every day and don't mistake the illusion of progress for actual improvement.

Effective language learners understand that binge-learning is but an illusion of progress.

When you try to learn long lists of vocabulary all at once or leaf through a textbook, chapter after chapter, without giving the necessary thought to the information within, your brain starts a tally that addictively goes up with every leaf.

The problem is, that mental counter represents the number of words and lessons you've seen, not the information you can actually use, or even remember the next morning.

Binge learning is extremely motivating at the beginning, but it consistently leads to burnout when the rational part of your brain finally realizes that all this euphoria was, in fact, unjustified.

Tip: Study in small chunks every day, even if for just five or 10 minutes.

Have a clear goal and use the language for something you already enjoy.

Effective learners realize that you can't learn a language without motivation that comes from the prospect of using it in the context you're passionate about.

For example: If you love horses, include equestrian themes throughout your learning. If you enjoy scuba diving like me, include Portuguese-speaking scuba-diving sites in your learning. Some of the best scuba-diving sites in the world are in Portugal and Brazil.

Tip: Use the language in the context of the topics you're passionate about and the activities you enjoy.

Avoid having a closet full of unopened textbooks or a phone full of learning apps.

Effective language learners know that there's no silver bullet to language learning, so they don't waste time searching for it. They choose an effective method quickly and stick to it until there is a real need to change.

One mistake beginners in language learning fall victim to again and again is going on a shopping spree for learning resources only to realize that they are spending more time scavenging for new ways to learn than actually learning.

It's good to choose a methodology that works for you, but it's even more important to do so quickly and get back to learning.

Tip: Spend a week researching different learning methods, select one or two that suit you best, and stick with them until you've read them cover to cover or identify a clear need to supplement them with another resource.

Strike a balance between consuming the language and using it to convey your thoughts.

Effective learners value output as much as input and make sure to write or say a new word out loud every time they read or listen to one.

There are countless examples of language learners who spend all their time cramming vocabulary only to find themselves at a loss for words when thrown into a real-life conversation.

There are also countless examples of those who dedicate every minute to speaking to friends and blogging in the target language. Such students are often remarkably fluent in their specific topic of interest or when they speak to their usual interlocutors, but they can struggle to produce a single coherent sentence outside of that context.

No matter your ultimate goal, it is crucial to learn languages in a balanced way. Reading and listening to native material on a diverse range of topics will enrich your own expressiveness. Using new words and expressions you've picked up from others will cement them in your memory.

Tip: Dedicate as much time to speaking and writing as to reading and listening and try to regularly wander into topics outside your comfort zone.

You will often fail, so celebrate your mistakes as opportunities to get better.

Effective learners value mistakes and misunderstandings as opportunities to learn and improve.

Everyone remembers Henry Ford's Model T, but what preceded it was a very imperfect Model A. Ford's mechanics gathered real-world insight into all its deficiencies and fixed them one at a time before coming up with the icon of the automotive history.

The only way to improve is to start using new expressions right after you learn them, make mistakes, and use those mistakes to improve your abilities.

It's not a failure to use the wrong grammar or make a blatant spelling mistake. The only true failure is when you don't learn from the mess-up or use it as an excuse to give up.

Tip: Don't look at mistakes as failures but rather as immediate opportunities to improve your language abilities.

Always be attentive and try to imitate the way native speakers use the language.

Effective learners mimic what expressions native speakers use in a given context, how they pronounce them, and what gestures they choose to reinforce their message.

Textbooks and dictionaries are great at teaching you what's grammatically correct, but they can't guide you to speak naturally in day-to-day situations. An expression that would give you full marks on a test, and pass every spell check, may sound absolutely jarring in the real world.

The best way to learn the language as it is actually spoken is to put yourself in context with native speakers and listen carefully to what they say! Then note down the natural sentence patterns you hear and use them yourself.

Next time you're queuing up for a latte, stop trying to imagine the conversation you'll have with the barista and instead listen to the conversations she's having with other clients!

Tip: *Always be attentive to what native speakers say in any given situation and note down the sentence patterns they use.*

Let's leave this chapter by just recapping some of the major points made throughout this book:

- Something inside you has got to want to learn the language.
- Ignore grammar at the beginning and concentrate instead on learning new words.
- Work on learning the most commonly used words and forget about words that are rarely ever used.
- Make language learning automatic by listening, reading, and digesting the language wherever you can.
- And finally, find ways to make learning fun by reading new books, subscribing to blogs, translating street signs, listening to music, or conversing with strangers.

I leave you with the immortal words of Fatboy Slim: *"Just lay back and let the big beat lead you."*

CONCLUSION

If you have learned one thing from this book, I hope it is that the most effective learning is not obtained by trying too hard. If you fill your head with useless vocabulary and grammar rules you do not need to speak Portuguese, eventually you will burn out and give up. Just keep to the bare minimum when starting out, find what works for you, and stick with that until something more effective comes your way.

You will have gathered by now that learning to speak Portuguese is different from just learning Portuguese. The emphasis is always on speaking. and understanding.

Learn at your own pace; do not force it. Find your own way. It is better to go slowly but surely rather than rush. The tortoise will always do better than the hare in language learning.

My abiding hope is that by the end of this book, you will have found your own path to speaking Portuguese fluently and effortlessly.

Até logo!

BIBLIOGRAPHY / ONLINE RESOURCES

I have literally begged, borrowed, or stolen a lot of the content of this book, and I am indebted to the authors, teachers, website owners, app writers, and bloggers who have spent valuable time putting resources online or in print to help people learn a new language. I will list them after this brief epilogue.

I urge you to use the resources they have made available. Find what works for you. It may be a combination of all or some of them, or even just one. If you can't afford to buy their stuff, use the free stuff until you can. It will be worth it.

By the way, I do not receive any sort of commission or kickback for recommending any of the courses, websites, blogs, or apps mentioned below. The fact that I have included them in this book is based purely on merit. Any of these *helpers* will stand you in good stead.

I was lucky. I started learning new languages when I was young, sometimes out of necessity (just to be understood by my peers) and sometimes out of precocious curiosity. I was also - and still am - filled with wanderlust and spent my mid- and late-teenage years hitchhiking around Europe (without a penny to my name and devoid of any dictionary, travel guide, or even map). "Ah," I hear you say, "that's why it was so easy for you, but I'm an adult, and I have a million things on my mind and a trillion things to do. It's so easy when you are a kid. You don't have to worry about anything else apart from living. I have responsibilities."

Yes and no. Kids do worry about a spectacular amount of things, and a lot of their time is tied up with doing things they also consider important. What makes the difference with learning like a child is that children learn or assimilate a language faster because, one, they have fewer hang-ups about making mistakes and interacting with other language speakers, and two, they learn better when they are having fun and are interested. This is when they are seemingly picking up the language effortlessly. My aim is to rekindle some of that emotion in you. Stick your thumb in the air, hitch a lift from whatever resource gets you moving, sit back, and enjoy the ride. Make this journey fun and exciting, and you will speak Portuguese at the end of it.

- Anki (https://apps.ankiweb.net/) SRS (spaced repetition software) with intelligent flashcards.
- CoffeeBreak Portuguese (https://radiolingua.com/) Learn Portuguese on your coffee break.
- ConversationExchange (https://www.conversationexchange.com) Practice with native speakers in your area.
- Duolingo (https://www.duolingo.com/) Fun podcast for learning Portuguese.
- Easy Portuguese (http://www.easyportuguese.com/) Free and easy online course.
- FluentU (https://www.fluentu.com/en/) SRS app and language immersion online.

- italki (https://www.italki.com/) Online teaching and conversation resource.
- LingQ (https://www.lingq.com/en/) Online reading resource.
- Meetup (https://www.meetup.com/) Online language exchange.
- Memrise (https://www.memrise.com/) Memory techniques to speed up language learning.
- My Language Exchange (mylanguageexchange.com) Online language exchange community.
- stephenhernandez.co.uk (https://stephenhernandez.co.uk/) Free tips on how to improve your language learning and a free newsletter when you sign up.
- Portuguesepod 101 (www.Portuguesepod101.com) Podcast for real beginners.
- Portuguese Survival Guide Portuguese Survival guide: The Basics
- SuperMemo (https://www.supermemo.com/en) SRS app.
- The Positivity Blog (https://www.positivityblog.com/) Henrik Edberg's positivity blog.
- Verbalicity (https://verbalicity.com/) One-on-one online lessons with native teachers

Other books in this series (How to Learn a Language Without even Trying):

Learn to speak Spanish (without even trying)

Learn to speak Italian (without even trying)

Learn to speak French (without even trying)

Learn to speak German (without even trying)

Fiction books:

Nazi Lesbian Vampires

Inside the Madhouse and Other Tales of delirium

Reviews:

- Book: Learn to speak Spanish (without even trying)

Great Value For Money!

"Really helpful tips on how to learn to speak Spanish. It is money very well spent." *****

Kindle Customer

- Book: Nazi Lesbian Vampires

5 Star! Loved It!

"Take a short, 2 to 4 hr. trip inside a different take on the Third Reich and it's insane bid to use the occult to take over the world." *****

Gigi

- Book: Inside the Madhouse and other tales of delirium

Great Variety!

"20 great stories, well worth a read!" *****

Linda Almond

- Book: Nazi Lesbian Vampires

Worth a Read!

" Definitely worth a read!" I'm sure there will be more amazing titles from this author to

Kindle Customer

- Book: Inside the Madhouse and other tales of delirium

Love

"Love" *****

Dee Crain

If you enjoyed this book I would very much appreciate it if you left a review on Amazon.com or Amazon.co.uk, good or bad, as they are equally helpful.

How to post a book review on Amazon:

1. Log in to your **Amazon** account.
2. Go to the specific product page for the **book** you want to **review** and then select the **book** format you used.
3. Scroll down to the Customer Reviews section and then click on the "Write a customer review" button.

Don't forget to log in to my website: https://stephenhernandez.co.uk/ where you can sign-up for my newsletter and get the latest tips on language learning and updates on forthcoming titles and special offers. Also, please drop me a line if you have any questions. I will be only too happy to help.